Praise for

How Plato and Pythagoras Can Save Your Life

"Nicholas Kardaras's book recounts one of the greatest, most dramatic shifts that anyone could ever have experienced—not only from life at the top of the pyramid in New York's big city nightlife to rejection, failure, and poverty, but from a life brimming with vitality and energy to the very portals of physical demise. This dramatic shift had an equally dramatic conclusion: he came out of it a bigger and better man, through the unusual and prima facie implausible stratagem of turning to philosophy for guidance—to classic Greek philosophy, to be exact. And guidance he received; a whole new sense of life, existence, and purpose. His is an amazing story that's more than a personal tale: it's a story with vast and direct application to everyone. To you and to me, who also need to experience a shift. I recommend reading this book both for the mind-boggling and highly entertaining story of someone who made it through the biggest rollercoaster ride anyone could imagine, but also for the pointers it gives for shifting, for being, in Gandhi's celebrated words, 'the change we want to see in the world.'"

—Ervin Laszlo, author of
Science and the Akashic Field and *Chaos Point 2012*

"Nicholas Kardaras has undergone a perilous, life-and-death journey and has emerged with a story that must be told. This riveting account reveals the timelessness of authentic wisdom, as well as the majestic, infinite reaches of the mind."

—Larry Dossey, M.D., author of
Healing Words and *The Power of Premonitions*

"With wisdom and wit, this is an accessible account of Greek philosophy—not as a dry academic discipline, but as a lived practice of purification and enhanced awareness, with rich transformative potential for all of us. Readers will enjoy the balanced blend of science, philosophy, and practical and spiritual wisdom; and carrying out the experiential exercises can help improve bodily, mental, and spiritual health and well-being, allow greater access to a deeper and more meaningful life and worldview, and foster a fuller realization of our true human potential."

—William Braud, Ph.D., Professor Emeritus, Institute of Transpersonal Psychology; co-author of *Transforming Self and Others through Research* and author of *Distant Mental Influence*

"A masterful integration of mystical Greek philosophy and contemporary, cutting-edge science. Kardaras's lucid and engaging work brings to life the distilled wisdom of the ancient Greek sages and suggests practical ways for a saner and more fulfilled life."

—Kyriacos C. Markides, Ph.D., author of *Fire in the Heart: Healers, Sages, and Mystics*

"Emerging phoenix-like from the glamorous, seductive—and destructive—world of the New York club scene where he mingled with the likes of JFK Jr. and New York's rich and powerful, Dr. Kardaras discovers a powerful and transformative method towards wholeness based on the wisdom of his ancient ancestors. You'll never look at reality—or yourself—in quite the same way after reading this book."

—R. Couri Hay, former editor, *Interview* magazine; society editor and columnist, *Hamptons* magazine, *LA Confidential*, and *Gotham* magazine

How Plato
and Pythagoras
Can Save Your Life

The Ancient Greek Prescription
for Health and Happiness

Nicholas Kardaras, Ph.D.

Conari Press

First published in 2011 by Conari Press
An imprint of Red Wheel/Weiser, LLC
With offices at:
665 Third Street, Suite 400
San Francisco, CA 94107
www.redwheelweiser.com

ISBN: 978-1-57324-475-6

Library of Congress Cataloging-in-Publication Data
Kardaras, Nicholas, 1964-
How Plato and Pythagoras can save your life : the ancient Greek
prescription for health and happiness / Nicholas Kardaras.
p. cm.
Includes bibliographical references and index.
ISBN 978-1-57324-475-6 (alk. paper)
1. Conduct of life. 2. Self-consciousness (Awareness)
3. Philosophy, Ancient. I. Title.
BJ1581.2.K335 2011
180--dc22   2010045333

Interior design by Kathryn Sky-Peck
Typeset in Adobe Jenson Pro
Cover design by Jim Warner

Printed in the United States of America
MV
10 9 8 7 6 5 4 3 2 1
The paper used in this publication meets the minimum requirements of the American National
Standard for Information Sciences—Permanence of Paper for Printed Library Materials
Z39.48-1992 (R1997).

Philosophy begins in wonder.

—Plato

Plato the Greek or Rin Tin Tin,
who's more famous to the Billion Millions?

—"The Magnificent Seven," The Clash

Contents

How Plato and Pythagoras Can Save Your Life

Greece and its colonies, circa 550 BCE.

Acknowledgments

I owe my eternal gratitude to the Greek philosophers of antiquity, whose wisdom gave my life texture, meaning, and a sense of purpose. It is my sincere hope that this book may do the same for others.

Yet this book exists only because of the love and support given to me by my wonderful wife, Lucy. Without that love, neither I nor this book would be here. I would also like to thank my parents, who continued to love me and believe in me even when things seemed to be at their darkest. I was not an easy son, so I thank them for their resilient love.

I owe the most thanks for much of the content of this book to my friend and mentor, Dr. William Braud; he was researching and exploring the parameters of consciousness and human potential while I was still a kid watching *Star Trek*. Our frequent and oftentimes mind-expanding conversations led to many of the insights contained within this book.

Critically instrumental in getting such a *different* type of book published was my ceaselessly resourceful literary agent, Adam Chromy. He too believed in me and in the importance of this project and was able to sell my vision in a dauntingly challenging publishing climate. Many thanks also go to my editor, Caroline Pincus, who is an extremely good egg and "got" what I was trying to accomplish. I am truly very grateful to her, as this book has benefitted immensely from her wisdom and experience.

Finally, I would like to thank my twin infant sons, Ari and Alexi. They teach me each and every day how to maintain my sense of wonder at the world; they remind me of the importance of looking up at the night sky and asking, Why? If I had a dollar for every time their eyes sparkle as they ask me *Yiati?* ("why?" in Greek), I'd be a very rich man today. But then again, thanks to everyone that I've mentioned here, I already am.

How Plato and Pythagoras Can Save Your Life

Introduction

Human alchemy—that's what this book is all about.
                                    —N. K.

On March 15, 2001, during a beautiful spring afternoon, my heart stopped beating, and I died. Literally. Living a life of addictive excess had caught up with me. As paramedics and doctors furiously worked on my dormant heart, my life—or what had been left of it—drifted away.

Once upon a time I'd been a well-known New York night-club owner caught up with all of the self-destructive ego candy that that world had to offer. From the late eighties until the mid-nineties, I'd been the young, Ivy League–educated owner of several of the hottest and hippest nightclubs in Manhattan and Southampton; these were much-publicized hotspots that were frequented by A-listers like John F. Kennedy, Jr., Tom Cruise, and Brooke Shields. It was heady stuff for a middle-class kid from Queens. I was written up in the tabloids as "New York's Youngest Nightclub Owner," while the flamboyant George Wayne of *Vanity Fair* included me on his list of New York's "50 Most Fabulous People."

But it was all fool's gold. That type of life comes at a very high price; it's your classic, boiler-plate Faustian deal—and the devil always gets his due. Several years of glamour and fun were followed by several years of addicted hell that had led to my almost demise.

Thanks to the feverish efforts of those above-mentioned doctors—and after over an hour without a heartbeat—I was able to pull a Lazarus. But I wasn't out of the woods just yet; I was in a touch-and-go coma as I clung to life via a respirator.

My god, what had happened to me? I had gone from the bright lights of the dance floor to the harsh lights of the intensive care unit, where I laid with tubes and catheters shoved into every orifice of my body. Glamorous it was not.

But just how *did* a nice kid like me from an honest and hardworking family wind up such a broken mess? And, more importantly, how did I—and how can anyone—heal?

Well, any challenge can be an opportunity for growth. Death—either physical or metaphorical—can begin the alchemical process of transfiguration, the most powerful type of spiritual transformation.

After my post-coma resurrection, I was desperate to better understand the universe and my purpose within it; I guess that a near-death experience will do that to a person. I would go on to embark on an amazing and transformative journey as I discovered—almost by chance—the way of ancient Greek mystical philosophy, a powerful wisdom tradition that embraced the notion of death as rebirth; in fact, Plato even described philosophy itself as a form of "death before dying."

But what does that mean? What I learned was that the Greeks had discovered a method that can allow a person to "die before dying"—in effect, to shed the biological skin and achieve an expanded level of noetic awareness that can then lead to personal transformation—all without having to take dying to the literal extremes that I had.

Plato had even used "breaking the bird free from the cage" as a metaphor for the soul transcending the physical body via the holistic mind-body *purification* of philosophy.

These were very new and shocking ideas for me: that philosophy was originally conceived of as a holistic *way of life* meant to purify an individual towards transcendence—that, indeed, Greek philosophy embraced a *metaphorical* death as a rejection of the illusory physical world and movement towards a more profound experience of a deeper level of reality.

I had always mistakenly thought that philosophy was some sort of dry intellectual endeavor, an arcane obsession with semantics, written in impenetrable language in dusty texts that were housed in the bowels of some university library. To be honest, I had perceived philosophy as something dead, not very vital.

I couldn't have been more wrong.

The *lived* practice of philosophy as purification—as, indeed, a way of life—had been originated by Pythagoras (with a little help from his friends, the Egyptians and Babylonians). And in what came to be known as the *Bios Pythagorikos* (the Pythagorean way of life) a healthy mind, body, and spirit were nurtured with rigorous physical exercise, a strict diet, daily meditational walks, and lessons on ethics and character, as well as deep contemplative meditations on math, music, cosmology, and philosophy.

But because philosophy has been hijacked by crypt-keeper philosophy professors, instead of staying the province of actual philosophers, this vibrant soul of ancient Greek wisdom—much to our detriment—has been lost. Alas, in our narcissistic, YouTube culture, most people are more inclined towards self-absorption than self-reflection. But that's exactly why we need the long-lost depth and soul of Plato and Pythagoras—perhaps now more than ever.

How Plato and Pythagoras Can Save Your Life is my very personal effort at resurrecting the long-lost soul of Platonic philosophy at a time when, I believe, our society needs it most. It not only chronicles my journey of transformation, but also brings to life the powerful insights of the Greek mystical philosophers in a way that I hope is clear and accessible.

Even though I intend to make Pythagoras and Plato come alive and be accessible to anybody interested in living a more meaningful and more aware life, I won't reduce their wisdom to fortune-cookie philosophy. I can't; I can't reduce their method of transformation into bite-size fun. Don't get me wrong: the journey *is* a blast, but it is a journey. In other words, there are no shortcuts.

But, luckily, what Pythagoras and Plato did was give us a road map for that journey of consciousness expansion and personal transformation. In my efforts to honor that original road map, I'll explore and examine some of their core ideas (as well as some relevant background info and current scientific research that might actually validate their ancient worldview). I also include experiential exercises, at the end of most chapters, intended to help the reader go step-by-step on this cosmic journey.

What will you discover? Perhaps, as the Greeks had discovered, that there's more to the world than meets the eye; if you're lucky, you might even catch a glimpse "behind the veil."

And if that happens, then not only will the way that you experience the world change forever, but the way that you exist within that world will change as well. Because with that shift in perception comes a shift in *being*. And then—*presto!*—alchemical transformation can manifest as a personal reality.

What you might also experience (as I did), as a fortuitous byproduct of this transformation and newfound expanded perception, is a much *happier* and much more *meaningful* life.

And you know, that may not be such a bad thing.

PART ONE

My Personal Odyssey

But it's no use going back to yesterday,
because I was a different person then.

—Lewis Caroll,
Alice's Adventures in Wonderland

Tripping the Night Fantastic

We've all had pivotal turning points in our lives—those critical two or three game-changers that create an entirely different life trajectory: the job that we should have taken, the relationship that we shouldn't have quit, the opportunity that we should've seized.

My life-changing fork in the road came soon after I had graduated from college on a beautiful September evening in New York during the fall of 1986.

I had grown up in the gritty, pre-Rudolph Giuliani New York of the late seventies and early eighties, as the athletic, clean-cut, yet confused son of working class Greek immigrants from Queens. As a teenager attending the Bronx High School of Science, I felt trapped in the outer boroughs and insecure with my ethnicity. Frustrated, I searched for something *more* as I gravitated towards the liberating downtown Manhattan club scene. With the subway serving as my trusty chariot, I ventured into the brave new worlds of Danceteria, the Pyramid Club, and CBGBs. These dark and anonymous rooms, filled with throbbing music that made my ears ring and my heart skip, offered a magical escape from the tedious grays of my life in Queens with a strict father who worked too long and drank too hard.

After high school, I bounced around a couple of different colleges before miraculously landing at Cornell University, where, in the rarefied Ivy League air, I once again struggled with my humble roots. Still confused and full of self-doubt, I drifted without the requisite plan for post-college life that most of my classmates seemed to have securely in place. I remember seeing the *The Graduate* during my senior year and feeling a solemn kinship with Benjamin Braddock, the Dustin Hoffman character. I so palpably felt his ennui as he sank to the bottom of that pool in his scuba gear that I was tempted to jump up from my seat and shout, "I feel you, my brother! Stay down! Stay the hell down!"

Unsure what to do with my life, I interviewed for a job as an assistant buyer at Bloomingdales, the vocational default option for those of us who were aimlessly drifting. Surprised to be hired, I started work as an executive trainee right after my graduation in June, 1986. I quickly received a welcome-to-the-real-world indoctrination as I found myself folding slacks in the Designer Men's department while getting yelled at by a short, nasal-voiced department manager.

God, I hated that job.

Adding to my malaise was the fact that I was living with my college sweetheart, a rather lovely young woman who didn't miss an opportunity to remind me that I had yet to legitimize our union by giving her a ring.

It's fair to say I felt trapped. Stultified. Smothered. Unable to breathe. It felt as if a nine-hundred-pound Sumo wrestler had plopped himself on my chest as he leisurely picked at his soba noodles.

It's also fair to say that I was unhappy.

It was at just that depressing point in my life that I heard the Copacabana nightclub on East Sixtieth Street was hiring clean-cut martial artists to be doormen.

"That's me! Clean-cut martial artist!" I thought to myself.

You see, back in 1986, I was still working a post-Cornell, young Republican look, but I also had a black belt and had been a national AAU (Amateur Athletic Union) karate champion. Martial arts had been another form of escape for me as a kid. When I first saw Bruce Lee in the exotic *Enter the Dragon*, I, along with millions of other young men looking for an identity, was sold. Karate classes followed soon after.

Escape was also the order of the day when I heard about the Copa job while dying a slow death at Bloomingdales. Now keep in mind that this was the original Copacabana that was featured in the movie *Goodfellas*. The same Copa of that infamous 1957 Yankees fight and the same Copa that Barry Manilow immortalized in that annoying song. But by 1986, the Copa had transitioned into a Latin dance club—a *violent* Latin dance club. In fact, I would later find out that the doorman I replaced had suffered a rather unfortunate occupational hazard: a bullet through the midsection, fired by an irate patron whom he'd barred from entering the club. The poor guy was now forced to take care of his private business by using a rather clumsy colostomy bag.

You'd think something like that—or the fact that since that shooting, the Copa's doormen were issued bulletproof vests to wear underneath their suits and ties— might deter me, or at least give me pause to think. Hell, some of my friends thought that I was crazy to want that job. But I didn't care; I just wanted out of the house and that damned Sumo off of my chest while maybe chasing a little excitement.

As I walked along East Sixtieth Street towards the Copa to interview for the shooting-induced doorman vacancy, I had no idea that I was at a crossroads in my life. I had no idea that I was about to embark on a ten-year odyssey through the surreal world of New York nightlife—a journey replete with colorful wiseguys, flamboyant drag queens, self-absorbed glitterati, self-righteous literati, vacuous socialites, never-were wannabes, sleazy promoters, hard-partying musicians, synaptically challenged models, misguided misfits, corrupt lawyers, Haitian hit squads, and, of course, the ubiquitous drug dealers of all shapes and sizes.

Nor was I aware that it would also include drug addiction, overdoses, violence, death, betrayal, corruption, and back-stabbing.

I quit Bloomingdales soon after I started working at the Copa. Within three short years, after hustling and working to save enough money, I opened my own nightclub with two partners. Located on the fringe of the West Village and the as-yet ungentrified Meatpacking District, Horatio 113 quickly took off as a celebrity hotspot; we were booked solid for film premieres and record-release parties, as literally hundreds of people would clamor at our velvet ropes begging to get in. After our meteoric success at Horatio 113, we opened three more clubs in quick succession.

And, of course, there was the requisite sex, drugs, and rock and roll.

I would stand at the front door, watching the frenzied crowds vying for our doorman's attention; I'd walk through the club, stopping to do shots with Uma Thurman or going to the office to do lines of coke with the celebrity du jour. When rock stars like Slash, from Guns & Roses, got out of hand (as he did), I had security unceremoniously throw him out on his head. When sports superstars like Michael Jordan showed up with their entourages, they would come to me—lord of my absurdly superficial little fiefdom—to ensure that their self-indulgent needs were taken care of.

My world was so glamorous that even some of my employees went on to megastardom. Before he became an action hero, Vin Diesel was one of my bouncers; before winning two Grammys, Moby manned my turntables as a DJ; and before winning a Tony on Broadway and making it in films, Liev Schreiber worked for me as a bartender.

For me, a basically insecure middle-class kid from Queens, it was all overwhelming—and intoxicating.

By the mid-nineties, my life was spinning painfully out of control. I was strung out on booze and drugs. My personal life was a disaster, as my womanizing had led to divorce and break-ups. I had several pissed-off wise guys looking to clear up certain "misunderstandings." My business partners and I were fighting to keep local and state authorities from revoking our liquor licenses. And, the cherry on the cake, I had a Haitian drug-dealing gang called the Zo Zos put a contract out on my life over some rather unfortunate free-trade disagreements.

In 1995, New York State finally did revoke our clubs' liquor licenses. When the state authorities let us know that it was last call, addiction really did a number on me. Without the semblance of an identity or job to keep me at least somewhat grounded, I drifted off into an abyss.

By 1999, I was human by only the most liberal of definitions. I was holed up in the isolating fortress of my shame as I sought the round-the-clock relief of my little powdered confection. I got high over and over and over again to temporarily numb my shame and self-loathing, because I just couldn't stand—couldn't accept—the reality of what had happened to me.

But what *had* happened to me?

My glamorous, velvet-roped, VIP lifestyle was long over, and I was now a broke, physically battered, and emotionally shot train wreck. My life consisted of an agonizing countdown towards my next dose of numbness. Tick tock, tick tock—time never moves as slowly as it does when you're anticipating the next hit. Tick tock, tick tock—I seemed to be in a strange universe where even though the seconds interminably dragged on, the years seemed to para-doxically fly by.

Worst of all, there just seemed to be no escape. It felt like I had blinked and somehow woken up in a nightmare—a horribly *repetitive* nightmare. Like some twisted version of Bill Murray's character in *Groundhog Day*, I'd regain consciousness and still be stuck in the same miserable place. There seemed to be no way out of the bottomless trap that I'd fallen into.

I eventually came to accept that I was unfixable, that I was destined to die in an addicted flame out. Hell, I'd even roman-ticized the idea; "live fast, die young and leave a good-looking corpse" became my delusional mantra.

While I had grown comfortable with the idea of dying, I couldn't handle accidentally bumping into old friends or acquaintances as I crawled along the Lower East Side, looking for this dealer or wait-ing for that one. God, I couldn't stand seeing the impossible-to-conceal frown or the look of pity. Even if they didn't say the words, I could hear their thoughts in my mind: "What's *happened* to him? He used to be on top of the world."

I was also beginning to go insane—I'm talking *One Flew Over the Cuckoo's Nest* crazy. I would wander the streets, disconnected with reality, sometimes talking to myself. I became consumed with Howard Hughes–type obsessive compulsions—repetitive behaviors, counting steps, avoiding sidewalk cracks, obsessively saving newspapers and highlighting various TV listings.

Worst of all, there were the times, when the high faded, that I would feel as if I were in a horrible free fall. But unlike the sense experienced by the parachutist whose chute won't open, my disorienting sense of plummeting was more than just physical—it was existential as well. I sensed that who or what I was falling, forever falling, into some kind of dark and dreaded abyss, disappearing into oblivion. My craziness, my compulsive repetitions—they were just my ways of maintaining some semblance of structure to reaffirm that I was real, that I was still here. But it was a losing battle.

I felt I was actually falling—or dissolving—into nothingness.

And then my parents reentered the equation.

They intervened with unconditional love just when I needed it the most. I had been so ashamed about the sad condition that I'd deteriorated into that I was avoiding them for months at a time. Eventually they figured out the truth, but rather than scorn me or judge me, they offered me love.

I moved back home with them for a period of time to try and regroup. It was very humbling having to be back in my childhood bedroom after all the fancy hotels and nice apartments that I'd lived in during my adult life. There I was, thirty-three years old and a once-upon-a-time big shot, sleeping in my old twin bed, between my childhood *Star Trek* sheets, which were adorned with the accusing, frozen stares of Kirk and Spock, looking up at me as I tried to make sense of my life. But being back home also felt very nurturing and safe. After all the champagne-soaked VIP rooms, the blurry after-hours clubs, the grimy drug dens with all the decaying humanity, seeing my sweet little mom's smiling face every morning as she held me tight and told me that she loved me—well, there was just something very healing in that.

My parents suggested that I get into rehab; I assured them that I could kick drugs on my own. As first-generation Greek immigrants, they didn't know much about the decidedly American concept of therapy, so at first it was relatively easy to talk them out of such a silly idea as rehab.

Don't get me wrong—by that point I really did want to stop using. And I did really try. I could always stop doing drugs for *brief* periods—like a few days—but I discovered that *staying* stopped was an altogether different matter, and I continued to relapse. At the same time, I found myself in a debilitating depression. I stayed in bed for months, watching *Jerry Springer* and *Chips* reruns around the clock (since I had insomnia).

Not only did I not have the first clue about how to stay clean and sober, but I also was still an empty, empty shell of a human being.

My parents eventually began to sense that they were losing me, that I was going to die. Unbeknownst to me, they educated themselves about rehabs and the therapy process and then, once again, brought up the idea of treatment. Only this time it was more than a suggestion: I had to go, or I had to leave.

I can't say how or why, but I finally became open to the idea of recovery. Towards that end, I really did some hard work in rehab, working with my counselors and honestly discussing my issues, as well as connecting with a twelve-step program.

After rehab, I moved into a sober house on the East End of Long Island. That was an experience: twelve life-hardened, overgrown men in five undersized bedrooms. They were a mishmash of humanity that were from everywhere—from prison to psych wards—as well as a couple of regular Joes, who were all struggling to get sober. Living in such cramped quarters with such a wacky crew and having curfews and mandatory house chores was all new for me, but it was just what I needed. It reconnected me to the human race. Granted, it was the lunatic fringe subset of the human race, but it was a lot better than the addicted isolation that I'd been in.

It was while living in that sober house that I started reading again—voraciously. As a trying-to-recover alcoholic and addict, I began to realize that it was important for me to quench a deeper thirst. I was drawn towards books that helped me to make sense of things, and as I read books about philosophy and cosmology by Thomas Merton, Daisaku Suzuki, Ken Wilber, and Joseph Campbell, I began to realize that the emptiness I had felt inside was beginning to disappear and become filled with something deeper and more satisfying.

After a few months in the sober house, I moved back to New York City, where I reconnected with one of my dearest friends, Gary Lewis. Gary was a former bartender in my clubs and by far the best human being I have ever known.

Like so many others, he had moved to New York after college to pursue a creative dream, but wound up working in clubs and restaurants instead. A dead-ringer for Cleavon Little of *Blazing Saddles* fame, he was just the warmest, most genuine, most kind-hearted person that you could ever want to meet. He was also the only person—other than my parents—that hadn't turned his back on me during my descent. Even during the darkest period of my life, he constantly tried to reach out and offer his help.

Gary and I reconnected and became inseparable. During one of our many late-night coffee sessions, while trying to figure out the next phase in our lives, we decided to write a television series that would capture all the drama and pathos of the downtown New York nightlife scene. I now had a dream again, as Gary and I met every day to work on our creative project. This was a wonderful period of growth for me, as I also continued my philosophical readings, attended daily twelve-step meetings, and regularly hit the gym. Drugs and alcohol became the farthest things from my mind, and I was able to put together just about a year of sobriety.

Around this time I also met (or re-met) Lucy, an old friend I hadn't seen in almost fifteen years. The last time that I had seen her, she was a young, sexy, Latina high school kid, dating one of my best friends while I was still working at Bloomingdales and moonlighting at the Copa. Since then, she'd blossomed into a mature and soulful schoolteacher who had traveled the world. The attraction between us was instant and magical. I happily reconnected with Lucy during Thanksgiving week of 2000.

That same week, on Thanksgiving Eve, Gary and I had just carried two loads of his laundry up to his fifth-story walk-up when I noticed that Gary was struggling to breathe. When we finally got to his landing, he dropped his bag with a big exhale and looked very flushed as he tried to laugh it off.

As he opened the front door of his apartment, he mentioned that he wanted to show me something on his computer. He was still red and breathing heavily as we sat side-by-side on his new wooden computer bench, but he managed a smile as he lifted his finger with an exaggerated arm motion.

"First we turn the computer on!" he said as he hit the power button.

Those were his last words.

Suddenly and without warning, his eyes started bulging, and he started to make a choking sound while furiously reaching with both hands towards his throat.

At first I thought that this was one of his pranks. "C'mon Gary, stop messing around! Stop acting like you're choking on a chicken bone or—"

But then his whole body violently flipped so that his feet almost knocked over his computer, and he landed face down on the carpet, fully convulsing. It took me three or four seconds to fully comprehend what was happening. I mean, you don't expect your young and healthy, thirty-six-year-old best friend to start having a massive heart attack!

Then I jumped into action: I flipped him onto his back and started administering CPR while calling 911 with my free hand. I had been certified years earlier in CPR, but it's different when you actually have to apply it to your best friend. The way his face looked haunts me to this day. He was conscious and kept looking up at me, his eyes still bulging as he struggled to speak, yet no sound came out.

After maybe about a minute (but what felt like an eternity), his eyes fixed, and his body stopped convulsing.

I was in shock. I just couldn't believe that Gary had died in my arms, right before my very eyes.

"Gary, don't die! Don't die! Please don't die! Gary!" I kept yelling and pleading and crying as I desperately attempted to revive him.

But he was gone.

I relapsed at Gary's funeral. It was one of those horrible open-casket affairs, and poor Gary lay there, shriveled and cold. When his parents asked me to say a few words to the hundreds of mourners gathered in the congregation, I thought that I might get sick. I stepped outside to compose myself and to breathe in some of the crisp, cold Cleveland air before I could perform the eulogy. As I inhaled deeply trying to keep the vomit at bay, I glanced up and saw a red bar sign glowing on the horizon. Above the hypnotizing neon, I could make out the lettering of the cheap sign adorning the ramshackle building: The Wolf's Den. Perfect.

I quickly marched over and ordered three double shots of Jack Daniels. As the fiery brown liquid went down my throat, I instantly felt the warm embrace of an old friend. In seconds, my knees got the weak, rubbery feeling that used to let me know that I was feeling, as we used to say, *nice*.

My relapse would eventually lead me back to other, powdered forms of escape. I was determined to hide things from Lucy, but it was pretty hard to keep my little secret when she found me lying on the floor without a pulse two months after Gary's funeral.

I don't have any memory of what happened; I've been told that Lucy and our friend Robert found me unconscious and that by the time the paramedics arrived, my heart had stopped beating. After trying to revive me at the scene for ten or fifteen minutes, the medics didn't think that I was going to make it. By the time they bought me to Cornell Presbyterian—not only the same hospital, but also the same emergency room that Gary had died in two months earlier—my heart had been stopped for over forty-five minutes. When the ER doctor came out to the waiting room to tell Lucy that it didn't look good, she screamed at him to keep trying.

After about another fifteen minutes, the doctor came out again, exclaiming, "We have a heartbeat! I don't know how, but we have a heartbeat!" But he added that everybody needed to temper their enthusiasm because I had been a systolic (without a pulse) for over an hour; that meant that my brain had suffered significant oxygen deprivation. If I survived—still a very big *if*—there would very likely be significant brain damage.

They called in the neurologist, and I was worked on for the next several hours. The doctors said that I was very close to total organ shutdown, an always-fatal condition where all the organs just sort of turn themselves off and the person just fades away. Lucy was told that it was extremely questionable whether or not I would survive the night as I barely clung to life via a respirator.

I remained in a coma for several days, but eventually I slowly started to come out of it. I started recognizing family members and slowly started speaking—gibberish at first—but speaking nonetheless.

The neurologist told Lucy and my parents that my recovery was a one in five billion event—regaining the level of cognitive functioning I did was nothing short of a medical miracle. The only permanent damage that I still carry with me is significant hearing loss in my left ear, accompanied by a loud ringing—what doctors call tinnitus. Lucy calls it my little reminder to listen more closely, to heed what the universe has to tell me.

I don't remember any of my time in the ER or the ICU; in fact, I don't remember any of my relapse. What I do remember begins almost two weeks into my hospital stay, when I had been transferred from the ICU to the cardiac unit. Even there, I was confused and disoriented. As I looked out my hospital window at the East River, I was convinced—really convinced—that I was on a cruise ship in either the Hong Kong harbor or the Rio Grande.

When the idea that I had really almost died finally began to sink in, I became angry—not just because I had almost killed myself, but also because I'd gone to the very brink of nonexistence and didn't have a white-light experience! It sounds childish,

I know, but my whole life, I'd been intrigued by the whole white-light thing. Now I finally had an honest-to-goodness near-death experience, and there was no freaking white light! Where was it?! Where was my long tunnel, with all my smiling dead friends and relatives getting ready to greet me into the great hereafter? I felt that God was playing the role of trickster. First he killed Gary, and then he allows me to *almost* kill myself. He lets me live, but what does he do? Knowing my obsession with death and what lay beyond, he teased me; he brought me right to the very freaking brink, but doesn't even give me a peek!

As the days progressed and I further emerged from my coma, I became more aware. I experienced a sense of expansion. I actually started experiencing what some might call a type of euphoria. Now whether that was some sort of neurochemical byproduct of my near-death experience—an endorphin rush—I don't know for sure. But I don't think so.

I'd always been an existentially curious kid—a science-fiction junkie if ever there was one—as I'd often look up at the night sky and try to make sense of things. After my coma, all of those existential and cosmological questions from my childhood flooded back: What is *life?* And what is *death?* What is my purpose? And more than that, what is my nature—my *true* nature. Am I just this skin-wrapped biological container? Or am I more?

I was thirsty for cosmological answers, and I had the very palpable feeling that if I didn't quench that thirst, I was destined to drift off and lose myself in the abyss of drug addiction again. Only this time, I wouldn't survive.

How Plato and Pythagoras Can Save Your Life

Exercise 1

Who—and What—Am I?

This first contemplative exercise deals with our own **self-understanding.** Oftentimes, people define themselves by their jobs or their familial or societal roles. But that's sort of relying on descriptive labels when we are actually trying to understand something on a much deeper level. **Yes, an apple is a fruit, and it may be red; but what is the essence of "appleness"?** What does it mean to *be* an apple?

When you ask yourself the question **"Who am I?" what are the responses that don't rely on superficial descriptions?** In other words, perhaps when you ask yourself "Who am I?" **you should instead ask *"What* am I?"**

For this exercise, you will be asked to take a few minutes to ask your inner self that question, and then allow your below-the-surface consciousness to respond. However, it's very important that this self-directed question and answer be done as a seated contemplative meditation and not just a perfunctory verbal prompt.

Take the opportunity to **sit in a chair in a room without distractions** (e.g., a room without any TV, computer, or music on) **or to go to a quiet place in nature.** Sit in a relaxed and comfortable position, with both feet on the ground and your hands relaxed on top of your thighs; keep your posture straight with your eyes loosely focusing on a point several feet in front of you.

Now center yourself; begin to breathe in slowly through your nose and then out through your mouth. **Gently try to still any turbulence that might be occurring in the ocean of your mind.** Visualize a still and calm body of water as the manifestation of this calm level of consciousness. As thoughts arise, try to gently push them away as you **focus on your breathing and visualize the glasslike calmness of the water.**

After several minutes of this relaxed breathing, you're ready to go contemplative deep-sea fishing in the calm blue water. **Now ask yourself the question "Who—and what—am I?" Sit still for several more minutes and become aware of what arises in your consciousness.**

When you're done, sit for several more moments and become aware of how you feel. Now look around the room again; do you experience it any differently? **Feel free to write down any of these initial thoughts and feelings,** as doing so will help you to process this experience.

2

The Journey Home

When I was released from the hospital, I immersed myself deeper than ever before into a spiritual and philosophical quest. I read more and more about philosophy, cosmology, and comparative religion, as well physics, metaphysics, and consciousness research.

While I had been raised as a Greek Orthodox Christian, somewhere between attending Cornell and becoming a nightclub owner, I lost my religion. In the smug, cocktail-party quasi-intellectualism of the Ivy League and the morally ambiguous world of velvet ropes and champagne, I became an atheist-leaning agnostic. But after the good old-fashioned existential ass-kicking that I'd received, I became more open to the idea of a spiritual dimension.

I felt compelled to read and research as much as I could in order to build the intellectual framework for a better understanding of what some might call the metaphysical. While the essence of the metaphysical or mystical quest isn't intellectual, but experiential, I do believe one can till the intellectual soil to prompt mystical fruit to blossom, and that through intellectual understanding, a person can create the necessary receptive conditions for consciousness to expand. What I needed was an intellectual framework that could allow for the belief in the *possibility* of a metaphysical reality. And once I created that necessary climate in my own mind, my own personal transcendence could become possible. But in order to make *that* happen, I needed an experiential practice.

Towards that end, I started doing seated breathing and insight meditations. I would take mindfulness walks, my goal always being an expansion of my individualized self towards the larger Self.

I also realized that maybe I needed to move out of New York City. I'll always consider myself a New Yorker, but I needed a quieter setting that might lend itself more towards this new, self-reflective journey that I was on. After discussing a few options, Lucy and I packed up and headed to the quiet and idyllic North Fork of Long Island, about a two-hour drive east of New York City. We moved into a cute little rental cottage a block from the beach in August, 2001.

After what I'd been through, the setting was just what the doctor ordered. It was a peaceful and beautiful green oasis surrounded by water: the Peconic Bay on the south, the Long Island Sound to the north, and the Atlantic Ocean to the east, with dozens of inlets and estuaries throughout.

In hindsight, there was quite a bit more to my move than my just wanting to escape the craziness of New York. I felt almost a magnetic pull to somewhere closer to nature, and my inner voice was also telling me that I needed to be near the water. Years later, during my training as a transpersonal psychologist, I would learn how important it is that the human psyche have a strong connection to nature and the natural world; indeed, the root cause of many of our neuroses—both personal and societal—is a disconnect with the earth. In fact, there are very powerful descriptions, almost two hundred years old, by Native Americans who describe the emotional, psychological, and spiritual anguish that they experienced when they were forcibly relocated from their earth-centered communities and onto reservations. One chief described how damaging it was for his people to not be able to "see the horizon," to be taken away from the earth and put into artificial "boxes" disconnected from the land. As the chief described it, many of his people were going insane because of this.

Most of us today are *so* far removed from nature that we don't even realize that our synthetic urban landscape is robbing us of our horizon; we feel stressed and anxious, and yet we don't even realize what the source of our discomfort might be. I may not consciously have known it at the time, but as I crawled out of my coma and began to heal my life, part of me knew that getting back to nature was a very important key to my recovery.

And as for water, well, many psychotherapists believe that we crave the oceanic state of the womb. Transpersonal psychologists don't view this urge as a regression, but rather as a call towards transcendence. In this view, the oceanic state is really an expanded level of consciousness; thus, a real-life pull towards oceans and rivers is merely a sublimated desire for transcendence.

Moving to the North Fork was, literally and figuratively, a breath of fresh air, and I loved that it was a region time seemed to have forgotten. Blissfully quaint, without the intrusion of big box stores or obnoxious strip malls, the North Fork consisted of farmland, vineyards, mom-and-pop shops, and a few antique stores. A traffic jam consisted of getting stuck behind a slow-moving tractor that had temporarily veered onto the main road. A bustling metropolis it was not. Life on the North Fork had a leisurely pace that was conducive to self-reflection; it was a place that allowed me the opportunity to breathe and to think. I instinctively knew that for my mind to be in a good place, the body that housed that old, warped cranium of mine also needed to be right. My preferred exercise routine consisted of long bike rides around the various estuaries and scenic preserves in and around the North Fork; on alternate days, I would also go running for about forty minutes.

As I biked or jogged, my mind would grapple with questions existential: How am I self-aware? What would this road or preserve "look" like if I weren't using my senses? Where is the essence of my dear friend Gary, who had died so suddenly? Where did my consciousness go during my coma? Why do I see through my eyes and not someone else's? At what point did I become self-aware? In utero? As an infant? Pre-utero?

These are the kind of questions that I would think about until near exhaustion. Then I'd find some secluded spot by the water to do a seated meditation. In other words, after tilling the soil with the physical and mental exertion of my contemplative bike rides or jogs, I would sit in quiet reflection and wait for whatever would arise in my conscious awareness.

As I'll discuss more in chapter 15, "New Science and Old Wisdom," meditating in front of a body of water has special significance. Bodies of water have fluid wave properties that seem to mirror a larger, cosmological frequency-wave effect described by some of the latest scientific theories regarding the nature of the universe (e.g., zero-point energy field, the metaverse, the Plenum Void, the Akashic Field). This cosmic ether creates what visionary theoretician and interdisciplinary scientist Ervin Laszlo calls a vibrational "wave medium."

By meditating in front of a small, earth-bound representation of this wave medium (i.e., any body of water), one can *entrain* with the larger vibratory realm. When two things entrain, they achieve vibrational resonance. (It's like the song says, "Two hearts beat as one." Or, as studies have shown, the brainwaves of advanced meditators can entrain, or become in sync, with those of other mediators in the same group.) In the case of meditating in front of a body

How Plato and Pythagoras Can Save Your Life

of water, the individual's vibration achieves higher cosmological vibrational resonance by, in effect, being "tuned" by the body of water, which is, in turn, tuned to the cosmological frequency of that larger wave medium, the liquidlike vacuum of space. (Note: If you can't get to a body of water, meditating with a candle has a similar energetic entraining effect. In that case, one entrains with the dynamic energetic life force rather than the liquidlike wave medium of space.)

But entrainment can only occur when person becomes *receptive* to the effect. And overthinking definitely mucks up the vibrational gears. That's why the interplay of physical exercise and meditation is so important. One can actively think about the existential questions while exercising (one can "seek"), but in order to tap into the transcendent universal wisdom and intuit the "answer" (not exactly the right word here, but language is rather crude when dealing with mystical matters), one needs to quiet the cacophony of mental noise (i.e., restless thoughts) in order to attain that cosmic entrainment. Thus, physical exertion can be one of several methods that can help a person to shut up and get out of their own way so that the universe can answer. Perhaps exercise and physical exertion also release any interior energy of the psyche that might cloud contemplative clarity.

Even though I didn't realize it at the time, my exercise-then-contemplate practice was entraining my brainwaves with those of the universe and rescuing me from overthinking. Turns out, it was also consistent with the Pythagorean notion of quieting the mind before doing any contemplative heavy lifting. The neo-platonist philosopher Iamblichus, in his third-century work *On the Pythagorean Life*, describes how Pythagoras and his followers would take long, reflective walks in the morning, before they were allowed to interact with others, in order that they might quiet any restlessness of the mind, "set their own soul in order," and thus become "composed in their intellect." After having done so, they would then engage in strenuous physical activity (e.g., running, wrestling) as part of their afternoon regimen of exercise and contemplation. On my own, I'd discovered the benefit of the Pythagorean notion of the "harmonic alignment" between a sound and contemplative mind, a sound body, and a sound character.

At the time, all I knew was that these reflective post-exercise moments were when my most powerful ontological and cosmological insights would emerge, when glimpses of transcendent awareness would manifest, or when the purpose and meaning in my life would become apparent. Something interesting was definitely happening to me, but it would take me years of further study and research to better understand it. Towards that end, I continued my voracious reading. Ken Wilber, Ian Stevenson, Daisetz Suzuki, Thomas Merton, Amit Goswami, Stanislav Grof, Huston Smith, Fritjof Capra—I read everything I could in order to better understand the nature of reality and the relationship between the spiritual realm and the physical world.

I also realized that, in addition to exercising, meditating, and immersing myself in the appropriate books, a critically important component of a spiritual practice was engaging in active spirituality; I understood this to mean helping other people. I initially got very involved with my twelve-step program, and I felt a sense of connectedness and purpose when I engaged in this service.

With my bibliotherapy, meditation practice, and service work, I was definitely growing—spiritually and intellectually. Yet I realized that for that growth to continue, I needed to pursue a *career* that could be of service. I wrestled with a couple of options. Eventually, I applied to and was accepted into the masters program for social work at Stony Brook University in 2002.

It was wonderful and amazing—after all that I'd been through—to be, once again, in a world where ideas were exchanged, to be in a healthy and nurturing environment, where I had wonderful professors who supported me and encouraged me onward. My mind—and the world around me—were alive with possibilities. At thirty-six years of age, I felt like I once had as an impressionable, eager-to-learn freshman at the Bronx High School of Science.

My first year in graduate school, I decided to get real-life experience working in the field of social work. After a short stint as a counselor at a homeless shelter in Southampton, I was hired as a social worker at a hospital with both a psychiatric unit and an in-patient drug and alcohol detox and rehab. I jumped at the opportunity to get that hospital position because it afforded me the opportunity to receive some wonderful clinical training.

Who woulda thunk it? This formerly addicted ex-nightclub owner, who had once made his living getting people drunk, was now trying to help get them sober. It was very surreal for me to be *working* in a detox and rehab after I had *been* to so many as a patient! But it was also wonderfully amazing and incredibly rewarding. I loved talking to those clients and hearing about their lives. And I think they might have helped me more than I helped them, because being able to be helpful filled me with such a sense of *purpose*—something that I hadn't had in a long time.

Over the next couple of years, I worked with hundreds of patients from all walks of life—college professors, cops, fire fighters, school teachers, chefs, artists, lawyers, clergy, construction workers, the homeless, single moms, retirees, teenagers. All of them had landed in detox or rehab, either willingly or unwillingly, due to their struggles with the great equalizer: addiction. As part of my job, I facilitated groups, did individual counseling, conducted lectures, created treatment and discharge plans, and facilitated family sessions. But, most importantly, I did my best to be as authentic, present, and compassionate as I could be.

As wonderful and gratifying as it felt to be back in school and working as a social worker, something was still missing. Still seeking to quench my metaphysical thirst, I enrolled in a progressive doctoral program in transpersonal psychology immediately after I completed my master's degree in social work. Transpersonal (literally "beyond the personal") psychology pushes the boundaries of traditional psychology and explores the intersection between psychology, philosophy, comparative religions, and consciousness research—all subject areas that I was greatly interested in.

But my real life-changing discovery came in the summer of 2003, while Lucy and I were traveling through Greece. (We had gotten married the previous December.) While browsing through a tiny, cluttered bookstore on the island of Mykonos, I chanced upon a little book called *God and the Evolving Universe* by Michael Murphy and James Redfield. In this fascinating book, Murphy and Redfield give a brief overview of the history of human development and describe what they call the "Greek Miracle" of ancient philosophy.

The words seemed to jump out at me as I sat on a whitewashed wall in the Mediterranean sun, devouring the book. A wave of knowing rushed over me. In the land of my ancestors, the doorway to the ancient Greeks burst open. I realized that my journey home had already begun; I had been living the *Bios Pythagorikos* (Pythag-

How Plato and Pythagoras Can Save Your Life

orean way of life) without even realizing it! The more that I read, the more that I felt doors of awareness being kicked open.

This increasing level of awareness became part of a process that not only helped me make sense of the world—and my place in it—but also allowed me brief glimpses behind the veil of physical reality and into the realm of the mystic. As the Greek metaphysicians understood, once the numinous is glimpsed, nothing can ever be the same again—including the person doing the glimpsing.

Back in the States, I started my Ph.D. program while getting my hands on as many books on Greek mystical philosophy as I could. Now that I had a sense that my contemplative practice (biking/ cosmological contemplation/ethical living) shared a bloodline with Pythagoras and Plato, I immersed myself even more deeply into it.

When it came time to develop a proposal for my doctoral thesis, my initial thought was to write a theoretical dissertation exploring the ontology of consciousness; after all, my contemplative practice had led me to many interesting insights. But then I realized that I was not only gaining an elevated sense of awareness—what people in my field call an increased sense of "transpersonal awareness"—but I was also feeling much happier and, to my surprise, becoming a better person.

I began to realize that when you are immersed in such contemplative and existential exploration, you necessarily begin to align your actions to be in harmony with those transpersonal insights—insights very often related to your higher purpose. In fact, according to Pythagoras, you could not only align with your higher purpose, but also actually merge with and *become* the object of your contemplation. In other words, if you contemplated the nature of infinity, you *became* infinite.

Interestingly, the more I read about the lives and wisdom of enlightened souls like Plato and Pythagoras, the more I began to find myself emulating them in true "What would Plato do?" fashion. Not so shockingly, I discovered that when one's template for an idealized human being was Plato rather than P. Diddy, amazing changes within oneself could occur.

With all of these insights and ideas swirling around in my head, I decided to take a long bike ride to try and sort out my dissertation. As I pedaled along a quiet, tree-lined back road, various thoughts raced through my head: ideas about the nature of consciousness, musings about what life in ancient Greece might have been like, thoughts about how conflicted and neurotic our modern world has become, and, finally, questions about how—and why—I survived my coma.

At the end of my bike ride, exhausted, I found myself sitting on an old piece of driftwood, on a cool and cloudy October afternoon, staring out at the perfectly still, glasslike reflection of the Peconic Bay. When the sky is right, the bay can create an amazing light show that can rival the best Pink Floyd laser light show; I stared in wonder as beams of orange and red light burst through blue-gray clouds, which then reflected a kaleidoscope prism of light off the crystal clear blue water. And in that beautiful moment of nature-inspired awe (and, perhaps, *entrainment*), the following thought arose in my consciousness: Bring the Greeks back to life. Revive the ancient wisdom of Pythagoras and Plato!

Since I'd been living a quasi-Pythagorean lifestyle, not only had my entire life transformed, but I also felt that my very *soul* had undergone a transformation—a transfiguration, if you will. So why not academically explore that process for my dissertation? Why not create a method wherein various participants in a research study can also immerse themselves in the wisdom of the Greeks? Since my life had so radically transformed, perhaps this method could be helpful to others as well. And if it were helpful, then I would need to let people know about it.

I'd been sitting facing the bay about two hundred yards from the New Suffolk marina in Cutchogue. I slowly stood up, feeling a deep sense of purpose about what I now was compelled to do, and I walked towards the marina to stretch my legs and look at the boats bobbing in the water. Feeling a deep sense of peace and inner calm, I noticed one particular boat that was a little more weathered than all the rest; as I took a closer look, I read the name written across the stern: *The Odyssey*.

I closed my eyes and took in another deep breath. Yes, I knew what I had to do.

At this point, some might ask how I can substantiate the wisdom of Pythagoras and Plato being so transformative in my life. How can I prove it?

This is how I would respond: the proof, as they say, is in the pudding.

I had been a morally compromised, horribly addicted former nightclub owner who had lost everything; I'd been broke, homeless, physically shot, emotionally devastated, and spiritually bankrupt. Post-Pythagoras and Plato, I've been clean and sober for a decade.

I'm a respected college professor and a caring psychotherapist. I not only specialize in treating addiction, but I also teach graduate-level coursework on the subject at my alma mater, Stony Brook University, where I'm a clinical assistant professor. And I'm an adjunct professor at my other alma mater, the Institute of Transpersonal Psychology (ITP), where I teach in the doctoral program. In my private practice as a psychotherapist, I cover the entire therapeutic gamut: I work with the addicted and the existentially seeking; I help alienated teenagers as well as angry couples; I provide therapy for those with significant psychiatric disorders as well as for those that we call "the worried well." In short, I work with every flavor of mental illness (and wellness). For several years, I've also worked in a school district, counseling teens that are struggling to find their way.

More important than all of that, I'm a loving and devoted husband as well as a caring and adoring father (of identical twin boys). I've become a person whom people in my community can trust and rely upon as I try my best to lead an honest and ethical life.

So I think that it's fair to say that I've transformed.

But here's the thing, and I think that it's a very important point. Personal well-being and happiness is just a byproduct of Greek mystical philosophy and not the actual goal itself. Just as stress reduction is a fortuitous byproduct rather than the actual goal of classical Eastern meditation, so too is personal well-being just a happy side effect of my Greek-influenced method.

So what was (is) the intended goal? The mystical experience, or "mystical union" with the infinite (the Greek *theosis*). The metaphysically oriented ancient Greek philosophers (such as Pythagoras, Plato, and Plotinus) wanted to break free from the cage of the physical body in order to experience—and join with—the numinous.

But to do that, a person needs to have a well-tuned instrument, to borrow Pythagoras's musical analogy. In order to be in harmony with the universe, a person's consciousness and body have to be tuned through a healthy lifestyle and through consciousness-expanding meditations. So these philosophers

How Plato and Pythagoras Can Save Your Life

developed a way of being in the world that allowed practitioners to experience deeper levels of reality—levels of reality unobstructed by filters like our five senses or our cluttered minds. They believed that a rigorous, holistic practice of achieving a sound body and sound mind, coupled with deep contemplative meditations, could actually alchemically transform a person and elevate an individual's level of consciousness in order to experience the transcendent.

That's what ancient Greek mystical philosophy is really all about. It just so happens that doing all that sort of also puts things in your life in perspective. And when that happens, you tend to live a more esteemable (one of my favorite words) sort of life.

I've included my personal narrative to give a sense of the transformative potential of the method. The rest of the book is an exploration, as well as a how-to explication, of the mystical wisdom of Pythagoras and Plato distilled from my doctoral research—research I was asked to present at the 115th annual American Psychological Association (APA) conference in San Francisco in 2007.

So kick back and get comfortable as I introduce you to a couple of old (as in ancient!) friends of mine. But hold onto to your seats because we're also going on a journey—a journey that could be mind blowing, reality rocking, and life changing!

Exercise 2

Take Me to the River

This next contemplative exercise deals with the concept of entrainment discussed in this chapter. Recall that when two objects achieve entrainment, they achieve a vibrational resonance ("two hearts beat as one").

It was also suggested by theoretician Ervin Laszlo that **the entire vacuum of empty space is actually a liquidlike wave medium,** not dissimilar to water and its properties. The readings suggested that if we entrain with a body of water, the water might act as a tuning fork to entrain us to the larger cosmological wave medium of the universe.

First, take a few minutes to do some sort of physical exercise. Be sure to only do as much as your physical health allows. This could include **walking, jogging, or bicycling.** After **15 to 30 minutes** (depending on your health) of exercise, **find a body of water and sit facing it in quiet contemplation.** This can be a pond, a river, a lake, or a pool. (If there are no appropriate bodies of water, light a candle and meditate while focusing on the flickering flame.)

Sit quietly and observe the properties of the water. Are there any waves or ripples? Is it totally smooth? **Begin to feel a unity with the water;** try and let yourself merge with its liquid, fluid properties. As thoughts arise in your consciousness, gently push them away. Take several more minutes of sitting in quiet communion and resonance with the water.

When you're done, sit for several more moments and become aware of how you feel. Now look around you; do you "experience" things any differently? **Feel free to write down any of these initial thoughts and feelings,** as writing these down will help you to process this experience.

PART TWO

The Being Human

As far as we can discern, the sole purpose of
human existence is to kindle a light
in the darkness of mere being.

—Carl Jung,
Memories, Dreams, Reflections

If I could tell you what it meant,
there would be no point in dancing it.

—Isadora Duncan

Just as in earthly life lovers long for the moment
when they are able to breathe forth their love
for each other, to let their souls blend in a soft
whisper, so the mystic longs for the moment when
in prayer he can, as it were, creep into God.

—Soren Kierkegaard, *Either/Or*

3

White Crows:
Mystics, Savants, and Other
Harbingers of Human Potential

All you need is "one white crow."

That was the sentiment expressed by William James, the nineteenth-century Harvard psychologist and philosopher who had also been trained as a medical doctor. James is widely considered to be not only one of the founders of the very sober philosophical system known as American Pragmatism, but also one of the leading minds of the modern era to have explored mysticism, spiritualism, and religious experience.

Pragmatism is the no-nonsense school of thought based on the notion that only those philosophical principles or truths that can be demonstrated by practical use or utility deserve intelligent consideration. Yet James was converted to a belief in unusual, credulity-straining psychic phenomena to such a degree that he became one of the founding members of the American Society for Psychical Research (ASPR). So how does a no-nonsense pragmatist become a convert to the world of clairvoyants, spirits, and things that go bump in the night? James's seemingly impossible conversion was the result of his encounter with a quiet, nondescript Boston housewife named Leonora Piper, an unassuming woman who demonstrated extraordinary and unexplainable abilities time and again under very controlled circumstances. James felt that these unusual abilities required us to reexamine our understanding of what it means to be human.

In his efforts to better understand the human condition and, indeed, our human potential, James believed that scientific exploration should focus on the exceptional—the outlier—and not on the hump of the bell curve; it's the exceptional person with anomalous or unusual abilities that shines a light in the darkness and lets us know what's possible. When asked about his interest in Piper and her abilities, James explained that she was "the one white crow that proves that not all crows are black."

Just as it's a waste of time and resources to look for the possibility of a white crow by studying a million black crows, it's a futile, quixotic quest to search for clues to human potential the way mainstream psychology does: in pathology and least-common-denominator approaches driven by volume-based quantitative methodologies. Because, as James believed, all you need is one single paradigm-shaking outlier.

It's the outlier—the white crow—that lets us know what's possible. Don't tell me about the masses or blather on about disorders; instead, tell me what I'm capable of! Tell me—show me—the white crows!

But what do James's white crows have to do with Greek philosophy? Answer: The enigmatic ancient Greek mystics *were* white crows as they pushed the boundary of human capability to logic-defying limits. Philosophers like Pythagoras were able to intuit aspects of the universe that are being validated by today's science while also being seemingly imbued with supernormal abilities of mind and body.

How Plato and Pythagoras Can Save Your Life

However, as I'll elaborate in more detail later, *belief* in the possibility of our own potential is key; without that, doors of experience slam shut. As Pythagoras said, "[R]emember to be disposed to believe, for these are the nerves of wisdom." To become a white crow, one needs to believe in white crows; for alchemical transformation to occur, one needs to be open to the *possibility* of our *possibilities*.

So let's then open the door of possibility by meeting some modern-day white crows.

It's 2004, and Daniel Tammet sits in a chair and looks straight ahead; he takes a sip of water and, with the cameras rolling, he begins to recite the numbers in a soft and steady voice:

3.14159265358979323846264338327950288419716939937510582097494459230781640628620899862803482534211706798214808651328230664709384460955058223172535940812848111745028410270193852110555964462294895493038196441...

Tammet was attempting to do something that fewer than a handful of people in the world can do: accurately recite the infinitely long numerical value of pi to thousands of decimal places without the use of any electronic or mechanical devices. As he sat and calmly recited the incomprehensibly long sequence of numbers, the only tool at his disposal was his incredible mind.

Meet Daniel Tammet, math savant.

As he recites number after number, the thin bespectacled man occasionally pauses to sip from his bottle of water and then continues once again. In the background, mathematicians from Oxford are furiously attempting to double-check his math with the aid of computer-generated printouts. As the afternoon wears on, Tammet, like the Energizer Bunny, keeps going and going and going. The small crowd gathered at Oxford's Museum of the History of Science is amazed; how can this slight young Englishman in his early twenties be doing such an amazing feat? How is it possible for any human being to correctly recite the value of pi to so many thousands of decimal places?

Pi is considered a transcendental number; to remind those who have forgotten their basic algebra, it's the ratio of the circumference to the diameter of a circle and can be calculated by dividing the circumference of any circle by its diameter. The resulting number is a mathematical constant that's represented by an infinitely long irrational number. That means that it can't be expressed exactly as a fraction, but is instead a decimal representation of a series of never-repeating numbers that go on for infinity.

As in, without ever ending. Ever.

In order to give some perspective on just how long an infinitely long sequence of numbers is, consider this: If you started methodically writing the ratio for pi at a rate of one digit per second from now until the universe slowly died out billions of years from now, you'd barely make a dent in (the) pi. In fact, if we wrote a digit per second for, say, 10 billion years, we'd have 315,360,000,000,000,000 digits, which would give us pi to roughly 315 quadrillion decimal places. While that may seem like a lot of numbers, it still wouldn't even be scratching at the door of infinity.

The first computer calculation of pi occurred in 1949 on a humongous machine that weighed over thirty tons; it took seventy hours of calculating on that house-sized computer to calculate pi to a measly 2,037 decimal places. More recently, in 2002, and aided by the explosion of computer technology, Yasumasa

Kanada at the University of Toronto was able to calculate pi to more than one trillion decimal places. And even *that's* still not close to the pi promised land.

How far was Daniel Tammet able to go? At his demonstration at Oxford in 2004, he quit from exhaustion after over five straight hours—and after having recited pi without a single error to 22,514 decimal places. While that may be a drop in the pi bucket, it was over ten times what that thirty-ton computer needed seventy hours to calculate in 1949. And when you consider that the average person has a difficult time reciting twenty non-repeating numbers, 22,514 digits seems absolutely mind-boggling.

When asked how he did it, Tammet replied that the numbers "appear in the landscape of my mind."

The world of savants is full of white crows like Tammet.

Renowned educator, visionary and author Joseph Chilton Pearce, in his groundbreaking book *Evolutions End* (1993), describes the amazing abilities of George and Clarence, who were what's known as calendrical savants. The two brothers weren't able to do the simplest arithmetic and couldn't even take care of themselves. (They had been institutionalized since age seven.) Yet they could tell you the day of the week for any given date up to *40,000 years into the future or 40,000 years into the past.*

Yes, you might be saying, "I've seen savants like that on *60 Minutes* or *Nova*; they can stutter out the day of the week for any given date, but so what? They might have a dynamite memory, but is that really so special?"

Well, yes, actually, it is. Because it's quite a bit more than just an amazing memory. The brothers are not regurgitating information from calendars that they had *memorized*; Clarence and

George haven't been *exposed* to printouts of hundreds of thousands of months spanning tens of thousands of years. Instead, they just seem to *know* the days of the week for any date.

If you were to ask them, for example, when Easter would be in the year 12,010, they can quickly tell you. As Pearce points out, knowing the day on which Easter falls in a given year requires adjustments for both solar and lunar calendars, as well as corrections factoring in leap years.

Similarly, if you were to ask the twins the day of the week for a date prior to 1752—the year that Europe shifted from Georgian to Julian calendar systems—they would respond with the correct answer, automatically adjusting to the correct system. Yet when asked how they knew to accommodate for the change in calendrical systems in 1752, they stare with a confused look, incapable of answering such an abstract question. In fact, they don't even understand the meaning of "calendrical system."

But how do they make adjustments that they're not even aware of?

Pearce speculates it was the twins' childhood exposure to a nineteenth-century brass novelty device that was pivotal in the development of their calendrical skills. The gadget, with various interlocking cogs, could be turned to provide the date for a 200-year period. But this brass-cogged gizmo didn't merely provide the twins with dates to memorize; the device has a 200-year limit, while the twins had a 40,000-year past-or-present calendrical radius. Pearce believes that, in essence, the device "tuned" the twins' neural field to be resonant with a larger "calendrical field." The twins, living a drab and dreary existence and being of a blissfully uncomplicated intellect, were able to repetitively and intensely focus on the magical little mechanical device—and, in the process, a door to a larger transcendent realm was opened. From that point on, when asked

How Plato and Pythagoras Can Save Your Life

a question that taps into the "calendar realm"—that is, when presented with the appropriate stimulus that seems to resonate with that larger knowledge base that they're cued for—they have been able to almost instantly respond with the correct answer, apparently "accessing" information that they've never even been exposed to.

This *should* be impossible. But like all white crows, George and Clarence redefine what may indeed be possible.

Pat Price stares at a blank sheet of white paper.

He is sitting in the small, electrically shielded interview room on the second floor of the Stanford Research Institute's (SRI) Radio Physics building in Palo Alto, California, and beside lead researcher Russell Targ; the year is 1974.

Targ looked the part of researcher; a laser physicist by training (Targ would retire from Lockheed Martin in 1998 as senior staff scientist, having developed airborne laser systems), he bore a striking resemblance to Art Garfunkel—only with thick, horn-rimmed glasses. His research partner was Hal Puthoff, also a laser physicist, who received his Ph.D. from Stanford and had been involved in gravitational physics, having published several scientific papers on polarizable vacuums.

Clearly Targ and Puthoff knew their science; after all, Stanford doesn't just hand out doctorates at *Star Trek* conventions. But some might argue that on that day in 1974, Targ and Puthoff were exploring a phenomenon that was so on the fringe it seemed more like science fiction than legitimate science research. Targ and Puthoff—two academically trained physicists—were doing pioneering research in the logic-defying abilities of the human mind; in fact, they were researching an exotic form of psychic phenomenon—that thing most scientists put right up there with Big Foot, the chupacabra, and

Santa Claus. Only on that day, mild-mannered Pat Price was the paranormal subject that would make these two very intelligent men with doctoral degrees scratch their heads in wonder.

As Targ is about to begin interviewing Price, he starts a small tape recorder. Speaking into it, Targ gives the time and date and briefly describes the nature of that day's session. Then he reads aloud to Price geographical coordinates (the latitude and longitude) of a location unknown to Price; in fact, all Targ knows about those coordinates is what a physicist sent by the government to monitor the research had told him: they're of a "Soviet site of great interest to the analysts."

But Price hadn't been told even that; he was merely read latitude and longitude coordinates.

After hearing the numbers, the middle-aged and graying Price slowly polishes his glasses and leans back in his chair as he closes his eyes. After about a minute, he beins to describe what he sees: "I am lying on the roof of a two- or three-story brick building. It's a sunny day. The sun feels good. There's the most amazing thing. There's a giant gantry crane moving back and forth over my head. . . . As I drift up in the air and look down, it seems to be riding on a track with one rail on each side of the building. I've never seen anything like that."

Price then leans forward and begins to sketch on a blank sheet of paper on the table in front of him. In addition to drawing the eight-wheeled gantry crane that he'd described, he draws many other details from the site, including a cluster of compressed gas cylinders and a "large interior room where people were assembling a sixty-foot diameter sphere" from "thick metal gores," like sections of an orange peel.

How accurate was Price's description and drawing? You can judge for yourselves by looking at figure 1.

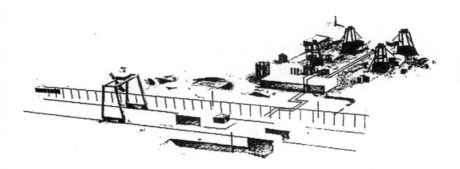

Figure 1. The real Semipalatinsk target site
This is a CIA artist's tracing of a satellite photograph of Semipalatinsk; these tracings were typically made by the CIA to conceal the accuracy of detail of satellite photography at that time.

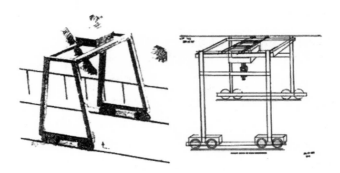

Figure 2. Pat Price's drawing
Close-up detail of the CIA drawing of the actual crane is to the left; Pat Price's drawing obtained via Remote Viewing methods is on the right.

The site located at the coordinates Price had been given were a top-secret atomic bomb laboratory at Semipalatinsk (in eastern Siberia), where the Soviets had also been testing particle-beam weapons designed to shoot down U.S. surveillance satellites. These very same CIA satellites would confirm via aerial photographs (see figure 1) the amazing accuracy of Price's drawing of the gantry-crane (which had been a very prominent component of the site), down to his drawing the correct number of wheels (eight) on the crane! (See figure 2.)

What about Price's description of the "sixty-foot-diameter metal sphere" with "thick metal gores" in orange peel sections? Because that sixty-foot metal sphere was inside a building, in a huge room, the SRI team wouldn't know just how accurate Price was until almost *three years later*, when further high-resolution reconnaissance satellites were able to catch a better peek. You can evaluate his accuracy as you read this *Aviation Week* article from May 2, 1977, describing the just-photographed site three years after Price had described it::

SOVIETS PUSH FOR BEAM WEAPON . . . . The US used high resolution photographic reconnaissance satellites to watch Soviet technicians dig through solid granite formations. In a nearby building, huge extremely **thick steel gores** were manufactured. These **steel segments** were parts of **a large sphere estimated to be about 18 meters (57.8 feet) in diameter**. US officials believe that the spheres are needed to capture and store energy from nuclear driven explosives or pulse power generators. Initially, some US physicists believed that there was no method the Soviets could use to weld together the steel gores [sic] of the spheres to provide a vessel strong enough to withstand pressures likely to occur in a nuclear explosive fission process, especially when the steel to be welded was extremely thick.

At this point, you might be saying, "C'mon! This has to be nonsense, right? There's no way that Price could be able to 'see' halfway around the world and accurately describe what's there in such detail, right? That should be impossible—and believing he can see something he logically can't makes Price some sort of a nut."

But these sorts of abilities *are* possible—for those very special white crows.

And Pat Price was no crackpot. Easygoing by nature, he was the decorated retired police commissioner of Burbank, California. In addition to being a seasoned and respected cop, able to deduce clues from a crime scene, he was also able to "access" seemingly impossible-to-attain information. This no-nonsense law-enforcement veteran was able to concentrate on a location and see it in his mind's eye—regardless of whether that location was around the block or around the world.

This ability to expand one's level of awareness to experience nonlocal phenomenon has been dubbed *remote viewing* and was the subject of the heavily funded government research at SRI ($25 million was allocated over an almost twenty-five year period) as the CIA had quickly realized the intelligence potential of such a skill. In fact, the 1974 experiment was *such* a success that Targ and Puthoff were investigated by the U.S. House of Representatives committee on intelligence oversight to determine if a breach in national security had occurred. Hauled in front of Congress for an interrogation, the SRI research team was soon cleared of any wrongdoing. After the hearings, and enjoying continued governmental support and funding, the SRI team trained U.S. army officers in remote-viewing methods. The technique helped locate downed military aircraft, as well as finding a crashed Soviet plane, which had been carrying a nuclear weapon, in Africa; this discovery would lead to a cover-blowing commendation from then-president Jimmy Carter.

While the very notion of remote viewing may sound impossible, the supporting data is substantial. Targ and Puthoff, after their experiments with Price, went on to publish several articles about remote viewing in respected journals, such as *Nature* and the *Journal of Scientific Exploration*. In chapter 15, "New Science and Old Wisdom," I'll discuss some of the scientific theories that might explain how remote viewing, along with other manifestations of nonlocal consciousness, might indeed be possible.

A handful of people, like Price, are just natural remote viewers. Price was the Roy Hobbs—or the Michael Jordan, if you prefer—of remote viewers, as he was documented to have an over 80 percent "target-hit" rate. In fact, Price is the only person who has ever been able to remotely view not just locations or buildings, but *written words* as well.

Unfortunately, Price died mysteriously in a Las Vegas hotel room two years before satellite surveillance confirmed the amazing accuracy of his 1974 remote view. But even before his untimely death, Price had developed a national reputation for his amazing mental abilities. In fact, his reputation was such that other law enforcement agencies would sometimes call for his services.

One such high-profile example occurred on February 4, 1974, when the Berkeley police department called Price for assistance in finding a young girl abducted from a very wealthy and prominent family. It was the sort of crime that focuses national attention on a local police department, as every newspaper across the nation had the story splattered across their front pages: *Patty Hearst Kidnapped!*

The heiress of the Hearst fortune had been taken by the little-known Symbionese Liberation Army (SLA). Desperate to solve such a widely publicized case, the Berkeley police decided to try the less-than-traditional psychic route.

Called the day after the kidnapping, Price, Targ, and Puthoff piled into a car and headed up to Berkeley. Upon arriving, Price asked to see a book of mug shots; as he slowly flipped through the photos, he soon stopped and pointed to a man that he had never seen before: Donald "Cinque" DeFreeze. Still pointing at the photo, he told the local police gathered around him, "He's the leader."

It was a direct hit.

DeFreeze was indeed the leader of the SLA, and Price would even tell the Berkeley police the make, color, and location of his vehicle. But it would be several months before DeFreeze himself would actually be found. Cornered in a house with his associates, he was killed during a confrontation with police.

Just how did Price do it? How did he pick Patty Hearst's kidnapper out of a mug-shot book? And just how was he able to describe in such detail the Soviet atomic bomb plant in Semipalatinsk?

There are many questions that white crows force us to ask—questions about who we are, what we're capable of, and, more fundamentally, what is the nature of existence? Because if what these exceptional human beings can do contradicts the physical "laws" of nature—the conceptual glue that helps us to make sense of our world—then what are we to make of a universe that we had so confidently thought we understood?

Kyriakos Markides isn't crazy. Nor is he a religious nut. A self-described skeptic, Markides is a sociologist and tenured professor at the University of Maine, where he's been on the faculty since

1972. As an academic, Markides has written and lectured on a variety of topics in sociology, ranging from political sociology to the sociology of mental illness to the sociology of international terrorism. But along the way in his academic career, Professor Markides also became quite interested in a very particular white crow named Styllianos Atteshlis, a Christian mystic in Markides's native Cyprus. Nicknamed Daskalos (Greek for "teacher"), Atteshlis was an unusually gifted man in his sixties who had demonstrated rather miraculous healing abilities.

Markides had been teaching sociology at the University of Maine for several years when he decided to put aside another research project in order to spend time studying Daskalos and his circle of disciples. The agnostic Markides had heard whispers of strange healings, along with other incredible tales of psychic phenomena, attributed to the humble Daskalos; intellectually curious, Markides felt compelled to apply his sociologist's lens to these mysterious practitioners of esoteric wisdom and objectively examine their alleged exploits.

What Markides experienced would change his life forever.

As part of his research, Markides witnessed Daskalos healing a paralyzed woman who medical specialists in both Cyprus and Israel had considered incurable; the skeptical researcher was in the room when the tall mystic simply stroked her back for approximately half an hour, after which she was able to get up out of her bed and, to her and her family's astonishment, walk again. Markides, ever the scientist, was able to obtain copies of her new, post-healing X-rays, which showed a normal spine, and compare them with her earlier X-rays, which had showed significant spinal damage only a week before Daskalos had laid his healing hands on the woman.

But how can this be possible? Even if, as Markides notes, there may have been some psychosomatic effect occurring, where the woman's belief in her own healing may have somehow enabled her to walk, it would still not explain the changes to her spine that the X-rays clearly showed—physical evidence that Markides academically trained mind told him should be impossible and yet, with the before and after X-rays in hand, was incontrovertible.

Markides would soon discover that these kinds of seemingly impossible events were commonplace in Daskalos's world. The charismatic mystic patiently described for Markides an energetic cosmogony (one that we'll soon see is very similar to Pythagoras's cosmogony) where "everything that exists is the result of frequencies of vibrations, including the composition of matter" (Markides 1985, 187). Indeed, in such an energetic and vibrational world, where thoughts and matter are essentially comprised of the same elemental "stuff," a well-trained mystic that has achieved mastery in that energetic realm could certainly manifest exceptional abilities, such as somatic healing or other types of matter transmutation. ("Matter transmutation" is just another term for alchemy, which, by the way, Markides tells us that Daskalos is also able to do.)

Over time, Markides, the skeptical social scientist who had maintained what he described as a "critical predisposition," witnessed firsthand so many unusual phenomena that his very pragmatic and scientifically based beliefs were shattered. What started as a sociological research study of Christian "shamans" by an agnostic professor eventually turned into a ten-year immersion in a world of unexplainable phenomena, which would subsequently lead to his conversion into a belief in what some may call the metaphysical.

Markides went on to write a critically received trilogy of books describing his experiences with Daskalos—experiences that forced him to conclude that "human beings have dormant abilities within themselves that extend beyond the five senses and that mind is not confined to brain . . . that there may be stages of consciousness that extend beyond the rational stage . . . that there are trans-rational stages of consciousness that mystics of all traditions have talked about throughout history and that what we call death is nothing more than another beginning, a transition to a different plane of life and existence" (Markides 2002, 4). In fact, when Markides was directly asked by a sociologist colleague whether or not he believed Daskalos had "so-called metaphysical abilities," Markides replied, "I will tell you what he himself says, and what in fact all authentic mystics say: that there is nothing really metaphysical in the world. It is the limitation of our awareness that would classify certain phenomena or abilities as metaphysical. Had our awareness been different, perhaps such things as nonmedical healings, psychic abilities, and so on would have been considered perfectly normal and natural" (Markides 1990, 9).

As Markides chronicles in his books, he experienced a shift in his beliefs—and in his level of awareness—based on his first-hand experience with a white crow; like William James before him, Markides found that a brush with the truly remarkable can be paradigm shattering and life altering.

That's precisely why white crows can be so important: they can become the philosopher stone in our own transformation, compelling us to take off our blinders and acknowledge our own potential. Once we unlock the confining box of our own perceived limitations—once we are freed from our own ignorance—we can then open doors of perception and awareness that the skeptically minded never even knew existed.

And, as I've mentioned, once the numinous is glimpsed, then nothing is ever the same, and *everything* changes.

How Plato and Pythagoras Can Save Your Life

Sometimes there are instances when a person doesn't become a white crow, but instead has an ever-so-brief momentary flash of transcendent inspiration (what in transpersonal psychology can be called a peak versus a plateau experience)—one of those wondrous and illuminating "aha" or "eureka" moments that seem to manifest in our conscious awareness from some deeper reservoir of wisdom. These magical glimpses can be life changing. The lightning bolt hits, blowing open the door of our potential, before disappearing into the heavens.

Let's explore some decidedly nonrational instances of expanded—albeit brief—moments of transcendent awareness as we take a look at a couple of people who have been struck by a lightning bolt of insight or transcendent knowing.

Imagine devoting yourself to a puzzle for fifteen long years without ever solving it. That's 180 months—or 5,475 days—of frustration. That's fifteen Christmases, New Years, birthdays—well, you get the picture. It's a long time to rack your brain over a seemingly unsolvable riddle.

But that's what the nineteenth-century Irish mathematician William Hamilton came up against: a seemingly unsolvable mathematical puzzle. Today he's known as a brilliant innovator who made important contributions to classical mechanics, optics, and algebra and is best known as the inventor of quaternions.

Now, most people today couldn't tell the difference between a quaternion and a Rastafarian, but in math circles, it's quite a big deal. For our purposes, it's not really that essential to understand the subtleties of what a quaternion is. Suffice to say that it's a way of extending complex numbers (which can be viewed as points on a two-dimensional plane) to a higher, four-dimensional spatial plane.

Indeed, the discovery of quaternions would essentially establish vector algebra and become a cornerstone of modern math.

The discovery of the quaternion was no easy trick. Poor old Hamilton had wrestled with the elusive secret of that mathematical formula for years. Finally, frustrated and disgusted, he quit. After fifteen long years, he decided that he was done tilting at windmills.

Saddened by his decision to abandon his quest, he asked his wife to take a stroll with him to perhaps lift his sunken spirits. As they crossed a little footbridge along the Royal Canal in Dublin, his lightning bolt of inspiration hit; the answer to the riddle of the quaternion appeared in his mind in a single, instantaneous flash.

Afraid that he might forget it, he took his penknife and carved the equation into the side of the nearby Broom Bridge. This little eureka moment is part of mathematical folklore; in fact, in order to commemorate this momentous event, the National University of Ireland organizes an annual pilgrimage from Dunsink Observatory to the famous "quaternion bridge," where, although no trace of the carving remains, there is a stone plaque to honor Hamilton's eureka moment.

"OK, so what's the big deal?" you might ask. Some mathematician figured out the answer to some arcane problem. Big whoop; happens all the time.

Well, no. It doesn't. At least not like it did for William Hamilton. Unlike our savant friends discussed earlier, Hamilton wasn't calculating anything, nor was he using his deductive reasoning or cognitive faculties to obtain the elusive equation. In fact, having truly given up, he wasn't thinking about quaternions at all when the formula appeared in his mind.

And here's another very important point: When the quaternion lightning bolt *did* strike his conscious awareness, he wasn't

How Plato and Pythagoras Can Save Your Life

even sure what it all meant. As he later reported, he knew at the time that he would have to spend another fifteen years making sense of that symbolic flash. In other words, the answer appeared to him, but he then needed time to understand it. It was as if the quaternion formula came, fully developed, from somewhere beyond his own intellectual faculties, and he was left to effectively reverse engineer it.

Let's take a look at another flash of eureka inspiration.

Today, we sort of take lasers for granted. They've become commonplace, found in everything from satellites to the express-checkout line at our local supermarket. But not too long ago—in fact, until just before 1957—they were the stuff of science fiction. It was in 1957 when Gordon Gould, an optical physicist, first came up with the idea of light amplification by stimulated emission of radiation (a.k.a., the LASER). Once again, it's not so much that Gould came up with a scientific innovation, but *how* he came up with his breakthrough that is a lightning-bolt moment.

Gould was lying about his house over the weekend, just relaxing, when—shazam!—the lightning bolt of inspiration struck without warning. Suddenly Gould saw in his field of vision a symbolic structure of such complexity and detail that he reported being "stunned, electrified" by the enormity of his vision. And, as it did with Hamilton, the lightning bolt presented as a fully formed, fully developed schema or blueprint in his mind.

In other words, Gould wasn't lying on the sofa saying, "Hey, you know, if I were to refract light with a mirror, then . . ." No, there was no incremental or deductive thinking going on here. Instead, almost like a medium channeling otherworldly messages, he had to quickly put pen to paper and feverishly scribble down page after page of the extremely complex knowledge that had appeared in his mind. Gould would say later that he was mystified that such monumental wisdom had just sort of magically dropped into his head without his bidding. But unlike Hamilton, Gould didn't need fifteen years to make sense of his illumination; by Monday he had sketched out the particulars of laser light-theory, an innovation that he'd later receive the Nobel Prize for.

The notion that a person can have a lightning-bolt moment in the form of a short-lived peak experience was an idea first developed by pioneering psychologist Abraham Maslow, and it would go on to become an important concept in the field of transpersonal psychology.

During Hamilton and Gould's lightning-bolt peak experiences, the seemingly transcendent wisdom they received took the form of mathematical or scientific insights; yet the lightning (or peak experience) that breaks open the boundaries of human potential can have another type of manifestation as well: cosmic consciousness.

R. M. Bucke, the late nineteenth-century Canadian psychiatrist who would go on to explore mysticism and write the seminal *Cosmic Consciousness* (1902), articulates three types of consciousness: simple consciousness (our instinctual consciousness), self consciousness (self-awareness that allows human beings to realize themselves as distinct entities), and, finally, cosmic consciousness, which Bucke describes as a new level of awareness that's at the pinnacle of our evolution.

During cosmic consciousness, one's individualized sense of self gives way to a merging with a larger reality as dualism gives way to an experience of the "allness"—the totality—of the universe.

Here's how Bucke described cosmic consciousness after identifying common traits in individuals who had claimed to have experienced mystical states (italics mine):

How Plato and Pythagoras Can Save Your Life

Like a *flash* there is presented to his consciousness a clear conception (a vision) in outline of the meaning and drift of the universe . . . He sees and knows that the cosmos . . . is in fact . . . in very truth a living presence . . . He sees that the life which is in man is as immortal as God is; that the foundation principle of the world is what we call love, and that the happiness of every individual is in the long run absolutely certain. The person who passes through this experience will learn in the few minutes, or even moments, of its continuance more than in months or years of study, and he will learn much that no study every taught or can teach. Especially does he obtain such a conception of "the whole." . . . Along with moral elevation and intellectual illumination comes what must be called, for want of a better term, a sense of immortality.

In her book *Ordinary People as Monks and Mystics* (1986), psychologist Marsha Sinetar refers to cosmic consciousness as the aforementioned peak experience; as she describes it:

> The peak experience means that the person experiences . . . the Transcendent nature of reality. He enters into the Absolute, becoming one with it, if only for an instant. It is a life-altering instant which many have described as one in which the mind stops, as a time in which the paradoxical change/changeless nature opens up to a person. The peak experience expands the individual's field of consciousness to include everything in the universe . . .

The instant of transcendent knowing described by Sinetar is that special moment when the lightning bolt strikes, when finite becomes infinite.

By tearing down constraints and limitations imposed by ignorance, fear, or doubt, human beings with exceptional abilities or illuminations—be they savants, scientists, psychics, or mystics—help us redefine what it means to be human. But what do they have to do with Greek philosophy?

Well, Greek philosophers were some of the earliest paradigm-rocking white crows. And the *mystic* Greek philosophers in particular were known to have developed rather exceptional abilities of mind and body. In fact, the essence of philosophy as practiced by Pythagoras and Plato was a form of human alchemy, a transfiguration from physical to metaphysical, an evolution from finite to infinite. Indeed, for the Greek mystic, the whole point of philosophy was the *transformation* of the black crow into a white one.

It's these white crows—past and present—that are the harbingers of our potential. As such, they are essential ingredients in our transformative alchemy; by showing us what's possible, they allow for our latent and transcendent potential to become emergent and manifest. For that very special reason, those exceptional beings known as white crows hold the key to our future.

But before discussing that future, let's journey back to our past so that we can better understand the ground that this transformative wisdom emerged from. Let's head back in time as we meet some of these earliest white crows.

Exercise 3

Mystic Mind (or How to Crack Open the Cranium)

This next contemplative exercise deals with **the unusual abilities of the white crows.** You will be asked to contemplate on how the calendrical twins receive their information, how Daskalos healed that woman's spine, how Pat Price was able to see halfway around the world.

But before we begin, **take a few minutes to do some sort of physical exercise,** being sure to do only as much as your physical health allows. This could include **walking, jogging, or bicycling.** After **fifteen to thirty minutes** (depending on your health) of exercise, **find a body of water to sit facing in quiet contemplation.** This can be a pond, a river, a lake, or a pool. If there are no appropriate bodies of water, light a candle and meditate while focusing on the flickering flame.

Take several minutes to try and **nonverbally conceptualize how the calendrical twins might have accessed calendars from 40,000 years into the future. Try and visualize how Daskalos energetically healed that woman's spine. Try and see if you can remote view like Pat Price did;** in order to remote view, **try and "see" with your mind the location where you are currently sitting from a bird's perspective, high overhead.** Take several moments to sensorially feel what this experience may be like.

When you're done, sit for several more moments and become aware of how you feel. Now look around you; do you experience things any differently? **Feel free to write down any of these initial thoughts and feelings,** as writing these down will help you to process this experience.

4

Wake Up!
Greek Philosophy Breaks the Trance

A funny thing happened around the sixth century BCE: the world woke up.

Woke up? Some people might ask, woke up from what? We didn't even know that it had been asleep. Well, in a manner of speaking, it *was* asleep.

Before the sixth century BCE, superstition and darkness reigned supreme, as dogmatic and oftentimes violent rituals were standard operating procedure. People worshiped a variety of gods—some nice and some not so nice—as they engaged in everything from animal and human sacrifice to other often very barbaric tribal practices. All of this bloodletting was an unfortunate byproduct of the way that people understood their world; indeed, before the sixth century BCE, the knowledge that informed the way that people perceived their universe came from hysterical and often irrational sources, like deified tribal rulers or mind-altered shamans.

All of this superstition and violence made the archaic world a very, very scary place inhabited by angry gods, insane demons, and even nuttier people. In fact, it might even be fair to say that if the relatively enlightened Middle Ages were known as the Dark Ages, then the pre-sixth century BCE was positively pitch black.

So, in that sense, yes, the world *was* asleep.

But around the sixth century BCE, things dramatically changed. More specifically, at around that time, at various points around the globe, pockets of the human species were awakened by a handful of enlightened individuals; these special human beings were the earliest white crows. This global consciousness awakening occurred in Europe, the Middle East, Asia, the Indian sub-continent, and perhaps in Africa and the Americas as well, although we unfortunately have less historical documentation from those regions.

Think about it: At around the same time that Siddhartha Gautama (a.k.a., the Buddha) was seeking enlightenment in India while sitting under a bodhi tree (for forty-nine days!) and became "awakened" to the Four Noble Truths and the Noble Eightfold Path towards enlightenment (which would become the foundations of Buddhism), in China, Lao Tsu was writing the *Tao Te Ching*, the scriptures that would illuminate "the Way," or the "Tao," of Taoism, the "mystery beyond all mysteries." This mysterious Way has been described as a mystical orientation that harmonizes the elemental forces of nature and the universe (forces the yin and yang symbolically represent). The Way speaks of the subtle universal force of *chi* and the practice of *wu wei*, a non-doing or "flowing" approach to existence.

And Lao Tsu wasn't the only transformative figure in China during this period; Confucius was also creating and spreading a philosophy that emphasized morality, justice, and sincerity. One of the fundamental precepts of Confucianism would come to be known as the Golden Rule: to never do to others what we wouldn't want others to do to us. Indeed, when Confucius was asked to define what it means to be human, he said, "To love your fellow man."

Also in India at this time, the ancient Vedic texts of Hinduism were unfolding into the Upanishads (which in Sanskrit literally means to "sit down near," referring to pupils gathering round their teacher for philosophical instruction). These Sanskrit writings teach the practitioner how to directly experience *Brahman*, or Ultimate Reality, which is, in essence, one and the same with the *atman*, or the highest self. Towards that end, the Upanishads introduced the ideas of self-realization, yoga, meditation, karma, and reincarnation.

Meanwhile, in the Middle East, the Hebrew prophets continued the earlier work and teachings of Moses as they created the Torah and Judaic law, which, in turn, would go on to inform our modern conceptions of jurisprudence. Now, depending on whether one has a theistic orientation, some might argue that the Hebrew Bible, also known to some as the Old Testament, is itself based on superstition. Yet whatever we may think of its theological veracity, there's no questioning the important foundational roles Judaic law and the Hebrew Bible have played in our Western, Judeo-Christian–based society. It also should be noted that the Old Testament oftentimes gets a bum rap for featuring a vengeful God, despite the fact that one of its central tenets, found in the book of Leviticus, encourages love and compassion: "Love thy neighbor as you love thyself." Those teachings from the Hebrew prophets would, in turn, inform yet another later important transformative figure: a barefooted carpenter from Galilee named Jesus Christ, who, with his simple message of love, compassion, and forgiveness, altered the course of human history.

And in Greece? Ah yes, Greece—something very special indeed was cooking in the land of Zeus and Apollo: Greek philosophy.

Philosophy—meaning literally the "love of wisdom"—was developed by a small group of enlightened Greeks thinkers who would revolutionize the way that people understood their world. Like lights emerging after centuries of darkness, these early philosophers embraced reason as a key to illumination and rejected the dogma and blind faith of religion and authority figures while pursuing a deeper noetic understanding. Instead of superstition and folklore, rationalism and logic became the means by which not only the cosmology of the universe, but also the human condition, might be better understood.

The Greeks' embrace of reason and philosophy was as powerful and dramatic a shift in human thinking as a thunderclap from Zeus and would lead to a consciousness transformation that has shaped our world to this day. The only problem is that we've lost something in the translation; over time, the original essence of Greek philosophy has been distorted as its transformative message has been all but lost.

But more about that later.

Buddhism, Taoism, the Torah, the Upanishads, Greek philosophy—all of these earth-shattering (and paradigm-shifting) lenses were developed in a relatively concentrated period of time all across the globe. This pivotal period in human history has been dubbed the Axial Age by the twentieth-century German philosopher Karl Jaspers. Jaspers had defined the Axial Age as being between 800 and 200 BCE, with the majority of the enlightened and axis-changing "paradigmatic personalities" (as Jaspers called them) concentrated around the sixth century BCE, the same century that saw the birth of Greek philosophy. It was an astonishing period when human history was turned on its axis as it underwent a consciousness metamorphosis that was inspired by highly evolved individuals.

How Plato and Pythagoras Can Save Your Life

These paradigmatic personalities were the earliest white crows; they created new ways of thought and experience that would not only transform the existing paradigms, but would also become the foundation stones for the world's major religions, schools of philosophy, and empirical sciences. As such, these transformative figures not only shaped the majority of the world's cultures, but they also created the framework for the way untold billions of people experience their world and the way people conceptualize their role or purpose within that world.

But as pure or wonderful as the original message from the paradigmatic personalities may have been, things tend to get mucked up over time. Messages get distorted, people add their own agendas as the pervading politics, and culture further shapes and influences the messages. As any kid who's ever played the game of telephone can attest, a message can become almost unrecognizable by the time it gets passed down from person to person (and in this case, from generation to generation). So a really beautiful, wonderful message of truth, transcendence, and enlightenment could fairly quickly turn into something else. At worst, it can morph into negative and destructive tribalism, as light can turn into dark, and then the perverted shadow of the original message can become the misguided precipitator for violence.

But back in the Axial Age, the message had yet to be corrupted; the light still glowed with a brilliance that the world has yet to recapture.

And while there were certainly different approaches and orientations that emerged during the Axial Age, the transformative figures of that period did have one thing in common: they were all seeking the way towards illumination, or enlightenment, or awakening. Call it what you may, but they were all trying to apprehend and experience the infinite mystery of the universe—

and in so doing, they transformed the very nature of human consciousness.

Since the focus of this book is how the Greek lens points towards illumination, let's travel back to the ancient Hellenic world and explore the origins of Greek philosophy.

Have you ever predicted anything? Have you ever picked the right lottery numbers or predicted who would win the Super Bowl?

Well, I would hazard to guess that most of you have never predicted what an ancient Greek named Thales had predicted in 585 BCE: a full solar eclipse. And he did it without benefit of a telescope or the ever-helpful weather page from his local newspaper.

Instead, Thales, a brilliant and well-traveled Greek from the busy port town of Miletus (on the Ionian seaboard of Asia Minor), was able to use his knowledge of astronomy and math to look skyward and accurately predict when the moon would cast its long shadow.

But in Thales's time, such calculation was unheard of. It was more common to consult an oracle or perhaps to interpret some omens from the harvest or even to sift through tea leaves in order to wean astronomical insight. Thales didn't do any of that; instead, he applied his ample intellect, using his logic and his reasoning mind to not only predict the shadow-casting eclipse, but to solve a variety of other natural and mathematical puzzles as well.

Now, some have argued that perhaps Thales wasn't the first person to be able to do such things, that he might have learned or borrowed those skills from his many travels to Egypt.

Perhaps.

Nevertheless, today Thales is considered the first Greek philosopher and the founder of a philosophical system centered in

Miletus—later known as the Ionian school—where he and his early students developed and spread these rationally inspired teachings, which would eventually become known as Greek philosophy. Thales is considered the first in an incredible lineage of Greek thinkers who learned to use observation and deductive reasoning in their attempts to provide rational descriptions and explanations of the natural world.

Several years later, on the small and rocky island of Samos in the eastern Aegean, a strikingly handsome, yet quirky mathematician and deep thinker named Pythagoras took this knowledge of mathematics one step further. He suspected that math could be more than just a numerical system used to count, quantify, and calculate. He believed the underlying rules or principles that governed numbers could also be the underlying unifying principles that governed the fabric of existence; indeed, for Pythagoras, mathematics was the transcendent light that could illuminate the innermost workings of the universe.

Today we consider both Thales and Pythagoras to be groundbreaking, early pioneers of philosophy. (In fact, Pythagoras—a former student of Thales—is credited with being the first person to use the term *philosopher.*) They were part of a breathtaking, consciousness-awakening movement that would also include names like Heraclitus, Parmenides, Socrates, and Plato (see "Timeline of the Major Greek Philosophers"), whose insights and wisdom would eventually transform the world—and our perception of it.

Yes, we *are* talking here about a bunch of dead white guys who, admittedly, in today's politically correct world are *definitely* not in vogue. But we need to give the devil his due because these Deceased Caucasian Men (not a bad name for a rock band) almost singlehandedly laid the foundation for disciplines like physics, philosophy, astronomy, biology, rhetoric, and ethics.

Timeline of the
Major Greek Philosophers

Seventh Century BCE

624–525 Thales, Greek philosopher and scientist

610–540 Anaximander, Greek philosopher

Sixth Century BCE

570–490 Pythagoras, Greek philosopher
and mathematician

540–480 Heraclitus, Greek philosopher

515–445 Parmenides, Greek philosopher and poet

Fifth Century BCE

490–430 Zeno, Greek philosopher

490–420 Protagoras, Greek Sophist philosopher

469–399 Socrates, Greek philosopher

470–360 Democritus, Greek philosopher

427–347 Plato, Greek philosopher

Fourth Century BCE

384–322 Aristotle, Greek philosopher

341–270 Epicurus, Greek philosopher

Third Century CE

204–270 Plotinus, Greco-Roman philosopher*

---

*Plotinus, although not Greek and born well past the classical period, is considered by most historians as the last great Greek or Hellenistic philosopher.

How Plato and Pythagoras Can Save Your Life

And the most amazing aspect of this awakening in ancient Greece was that, for the first time in human history, philosophers embraced reason as a key to illumination. This effort to better understand not only led them to use natural observation and deductive reasoning, but also prompted them to ask the big, existential questions. As they looked up in wonder and awe at the brilliance of the starry night sky, they asked questions like, what is the origin of the universe? What is the nature of the cosmos? Is there any reality beyond my senses? What is my purpose?

Unlike their predecessors, who found their answers to those big existential questions in superstition and religion, the Greeks tried to use their reasoning minds via philosophical contemplation to intuit the answers. Towards that end, Greek philosophers developed a systematic philosophical exploration of both *anthropos* (humanly affairs) and *cosmos* (the universe) that would eventually become the foundation for both the empirical sciences as well as for philosophical inquiry.

When discussing ancient Greek philosophy, it's important to mention that Hellenic philosophy wasn't just one happy homogeneous system; there were many variations of flower that blossomed on that tree.

We should also bear in mind that ancient Greece itself during this period was also not one large, cohesive, homogeneous, Kumbaya nation. While the Greeks did share a common language, culture, and polytheistic belief system, the country of ancient Greece consisted of various states and colonies that operated, for the most part, rather independently and quite autonomously (although they would often unite against common opponents during times of war, as was the case during the Trojan War and the Peloponnesian

Time Periods of
Ancient Greek Philosophy

Pre-Socratic Philosophy
   (sixth to fifth century BCE)

The Ionians (Thales, Anaximander, Xenphanes,
   Heraclitus)
The Pythagorean School (Pythagoras, Philolaus,
   Archytas, Alcmaeon)
The Eleatic School (Parmenides, Zeno, and Melissus)
The Pluralists and Atomists (Empedocles, Anaxagoras
   and Democritus)

Classical Philosophy
   (fourth century BCE)

The Sophists (Protagoras, Gorgias, Antiphon, Hippias)
Socrates
Plato
Aristotle

Hellenistic Philosophy
   (late fourth century BCE to first century CE)

Cynics (Antishenes, Diogenes, Crates)
Stoics (Zeno of Citium, Cleanthes)
Epicureans (Epicurus, Metrodorus, Hemarchus,
   Lucretius)
Skeptics (Pyrro of Elis, Carneades)

How Plato and Pythagoras Can Save Your Life

War). And since the Greeks were a sea-faring people, this ancient Hellenic world was geographically spread out, consisting of cities and villages in what is today mainland Greece, as well as along the western coast of what is now Turkey and the eastern coast of what is now Italy, and other colonies sprinkled as far away as the Iberian Coast and Asia Minor. (See the map at the beginning of the book.)

As for the various philosophical schools, most historians tend to break down Greek philosophy into three periods, with several schools or movements within each of those periods (see "Timeline of Major Greek Philosophers").

Broadly speaking, the first period is known as the pre-Socratic, creatively named because it occurred in the time *before* Socrates. This period begins with Thales in the sixth century BCE and ends during the fifth century BCE; the various philosophical schools during this period where the Ionian, the Pythagorean, the Milesian, and the Pluralist and Atomist. The next philosophical age is known as the classical period (the fourth century BCE) and includes Socrates, Plato, and Aristotle. The final philosophical age is the Hellenistic period (late fourth century BCE and all the way into the first century CE). In this period we have the Cynics, the Stoics, the Epicureans and the Skeptics, and Plotinus coming much later during the third century CE.

In very, very broad strokes, the tree of ancient Greek philosophy is considered to have two main branches; these branches have been described as the *scientific temperament* and the *mystic temperament*.

Again, very broadly speaking, the philosophers of the scientific temperament (which included the Ionian school, as well as the Atomists) favored observation and inquiry into the natural world. Philosophers like Thales, Anaximenes, and Anaximander became quite obsessed with discovering what the universe was made of and were thus determined to deconstruct it to its quint-essential substance. Sure, they got it wrong (Thales thought that substance was water; Anaximenes thought it was air), but give them credit for trying. And keep in mind that they didn't have any of our fancy, high-tech gadgets to work with. Instead, all they had was a rock to sit on and their agile and probing minds.

Now let's discuss the mystical branch of the Greek philosophical tree. This branch (which included the Idealists and the Eleatic school) was comprised of philosophers like Pythagoras, Plato, Parmenides, and other later neoplatonists such as Plotinus. They embraced the notion that there was an unseen "implicate" order of reality (reflected in Plato's Ideal Forms, Pythagoras's Informational Realm, Plotinus's "the One") that was unavailable to our senses; according to them, our crude senses were limited and able to perceive only the visible "explicate"—yet illusory—shadow manifestations (i.e., matter and the material world) of that deeper level of reality. In essence, they believed that the physical world was a quasi-illusion; ephemeral and short lived, and that our senses would often deceive us into believing that the illusion was real, when, in fact, it had no permanence.

In contrast, the transcendent realm, of which Ideal Forms were underlying principles, *were* eternal and everlasting, but could be illuminated only by the reasoning of our higher mind via contemplative meditations on things such as mathematics, which, happily, could reveal those eternal truths. Simply put, the chair you're sitting on will crumble and dissolve to dust, but two plus two is forever. And, *contemplating* that eternal truth can have an elevating effect on one's consciousness and a purifying effect on one's soul.

How Plato and Pythagoras Can Save Your Life

The role, then, of philosophy (according to the mystic philosophers) was to purify or attune the mind, body, and soul via not only contemplative meditations on such things as the Eternal Forms, but also by a rather rigorous and holistic lifestyle. This whole-person attunement would then allow the initiate to experience and apprehend that deeper level of transcendent reality. I'll let Hierocles, a fifth-century neoplatonist, explain it:

> Philosophy is the purification and perfection of human nature; it's purification, because it delivers it from the temerity and folly that proceed from matter and because it disengages its affections from the mortal body; and it's perfection, because it makes it recover its original felicity by restoring it to the likeness of God.

See what I mean? As Hierocles mentions (and as we'll discuss a bit later in more detail) this purification was meant to not only help the experient apprehend the deeper level of reality, but, in a sense, to mystically *join* with it.

Another way to describe this attunement as a means of mystical joining borrows from a concept in the physical sciences known as *entrainment* (which was briefly discussed in chapter 2). Entrainment has several different definitions in chemistry, engineering, and the biological sciences, but in this context I'm referring to the definition of entrainment as "an adjustment to an internal rhythm of an organism so that it synchronizes with an external cycle"; in other words, when something entrains, it vibrates in sync with something else. In this case, the mind, body, and soul of a person is purified by Greek mystic philosophy so that it can be in sync—entrained—with the larger universal rhythm.

What gets in the way of this entrainment are the traps of the material world, as we get seduced by that illusion. Using our mind to contemplate matters eternal (Plato's Forms, mathematics, God) can be the key to breaking us out of this trap.

That's what Pythagoras and Plato were all about.

Unfortunately, most people today don't know any of this. While they may have heard of Plato and Pythagoras, they have no idea that these Greek philosophers developed a transformative method that can help free a person (and his or her soul) from this illusory trap of the material world and the physical body, or what Plato had analogized as "freeing a bird from a cage."

Instead, like easily distracted children, most people are hypnotized by shiny little baubles like *American Idol* or glistening junk from the mall, while their souls get trapped—and crushed—further in the cage that Plato describes.

But before we further explore the liberating wisdom of Greek mystical philosophy, let's take a closer look at how philosophy differs from other ways of knowing.

5

The Ultimate Cage Match:
Philosophy, Science, and Religion

(or, Togas, Bibles, and Microscopes:
Why Can't We All Just Get Along?)

What is philosophy? What makes it different from other types of lenses—say science or religion—that are also used by people to better understand their world?

Allow me to share a little not-so-ancient parable that might clear things up a bit.

A chicken crosses the road.

Three men are sitting in chairs spaced about thirty feet apart, facing this poultry procession. One wears a wrinkled seersucker suit and sits leisurely in a bamboo rocker; the second is wearing suspenders that hold up very high-waisted pants as he sits erect in a very practical, black metal folding chair, while the third is dressed in a simple black suit and sits perched on a very uncomfortable-looking, austere wooden stool.

The suspendered man in the folding chair is a scientist. Ever observant, he uses his empirical skills to track the feathered fowl's progress as she clucks her way forward. He's observed some very definite behavior; yes, indeed, he's witnessed the chicken locomote across the dusty road. The scientist's mind is on fire as he deconstructs how this event may have occurred; he factors in laws of physics, motion, and inertia, as well as insights from the science of physiology, in order to better understand just how the little clucker is able to make the journey.

Finally, after a long period of protracted analysis and calculation, the scientist is dripping with sweat. But his labors have borne fruit.

"Eureka!" he cries out. "I understand how the chicken has crossed the road! I know *how!* I know *how!*" he repeats excitedly.

Next to him, the seersucker-wearing man sits in his rocker, casually sipping lemonade. He's a philosopher. He's also been watching the poultry parade with great interest. As the scientist continues to shriek "I know *how!* I know *how!*" the philosopher slowly takes off his jacket to stay cool in the blistering afternoon sun and reclines in his rocker, lost in thought.

Meanwhile, the man in black—a theologian—has been sitting quietly on his rigid stool. As the scientist continues with his excited claims, the theologian reaches inside his lined breast pocket and pulls out a small, tattered black book and places it on his lap.

The chicken finally reaches the other side.

The scientist is almost beside himself now with the ecstasy of new understanding. As he cries out once again that he knows *how* the chicken completed his journey, the philosopher has had enough and yells out to him, "Dang fool! The question isn't *how!* It's not, *how* did the chicken cross the road? but *why* did the chicken cross the road? The *why* questions are what it's all about!" And with that, the philosopher looks over to the theologian for support. "Isn't that right, holy one? Can you tell that dang fool that he needs to be asking *why* not *how?*"

How Plato and Pythagoras Can Save Your Life

"Why yes, my philosopher friend, *why* is indeed the important question. But we needn't ask it. We already know why the chicken crossed the road," the theologian confidently declares.

"Well, my holy friend, I've been sitting here all afternoon deeply contemplating just why that little feathered bird crossed this old road. And I've tried to use my reasoning abilities to get to the heart of the matter, but I haven't been able to," the philosopher says with some frustration.

With that, the theologian smiles a knowing little smile. "Why, the answer is quite simple," he says, as he lifts up his black book. "If we were to ask *why* did the chicken cross the road? I can answer that question because the answer is stated right here in this book that contains all of the wisdom in the universe."

"All right, holy man," the philosopher says, now getting a little impatient, "So tell me, *why* did the chicken cross the road?"

With that, the theologian looks deeply into the philosopher's eyes and quietly replies, "Because it's God's will."

As soon as the still-rambling scientist hears the theologian utter the G word, he falls right off of his folding chair and starts mumbling, "God? God?! Where's the proof? I see no evidence of such a thing! There can be no God without evidence!"

That declarative statement gets the theologian fired up. As the two engage in a heated exchange, the philosopher leans back in his rocker and sips his lemonade again. Now a little half smile comes across his face as he says in a loud tone to the scientist, "No evidence? No evidence?! Dang fool, look all around you!" as he gestures towards the beauty of the landscape. "Beautiful sunsets, dazzling flowers—nature in all of its glory."

He then pulls his chair closer to the scientist. "Do you want to know how else I know there's a God—what my other 'evidence' is?"

The scientist, who had grown quiet while listening to the philosopher, slowly nods his head, "Yes, what else is your proof?"

The philosopher takes a deep breath. Before he responds, he momentarily wonders whether the man of science will be able to see the obvious. Finally, he proceeds: "We exist, don't we? I mean, 'I think, therefore I am,' right? Well, how can we have just come into being from nothingness? What created the something—call it your Big Bang—that started the whole dance, that led to us sitting here and watching this feathered bird crossing the road and having this discussion, huh? Who—or what—started the whole ball rolling?"

The scientist grows silent for a moment, but then responds, "I still see no *scientific* evidence; can you devise for me an experiment that can prove that there is this thing called God?"

The philosopher just shakes his head in disgust as he answers, "I learned a long time ago, as a school boy, a very wise old saying. Let me repeat it for you: 'Absence of evidence—scientific or otherwise—is not evidence of absence.'"

With that, the three men erupt into loud, three-way arguing. This argument continues long after the sun goes down and long after the moon is high in the sky; in fact, even today, if the evening is very quiet and very still—and if you listen very, very closely—you can still hear the three men arguing.

The parable illustrates the biggest distinctions between the three lenses of science, philosophy, and religion: science explores how, philosophy asks why, and religion confidently asserts, "We already know why; it says so right in our holy book!"

Let's take a listen to what Bertrand Russell, who's considered one of the greatest philosophers and historians of the twentieth

How Plato and Pythagoras Can Save Your Life

century and who is the author of the classic *A History of Western Philosophy* (1945), had to say regarding the distinctions between science, philosophy, and theology:

> Philosophy . . . is something intermediate between theology and science. Like theology, it consists of speculations on matters to which definite knowledge has, so far, been unascertainable; but like science, it appeals to human reason rather than to authority, whether that of tradition or that of revelation. All *definite* knowledge . . . belongs to science; all *dogma* as to what surpasses definite knowledge belongs to theology. But between theology and science is a No Man's Land, exposed to attack from both sides; this No Man's Land is philosophy.

As Russell understood it, science was the search for discovery via observation and reasoning (as opposed to dogma), while religion was an attempt to explain the hitherto unanswerable questions: Does the universe have a purpose? How did it come into existence? What happens to a person after they die?

While science can often help shed some light on those heavy-duty questions, it's inherently at a disadvantage compared to religion. That's because science, with its emphasis on the repeatability of experimental findings and its guiding principal of empirical observation oftentimes limits itself to the aspects of a phenomenon that can be operationalized into a repeatable experimental format. But the answers to the big questions don't usually fit into that neat little box; indeed, it would be rather challenging finding humanity's purpose under a microscope or proving God's existence in a lab.

Where science *has* excelled, however, is in deconstructing phenomena into small subsections and dissecting and analyzing those reduced bits. In other words, science has gotten very good at explaining *how* the different smaller parts of the engine work, but it still can't explain *why* the engine was built—or who built it. Science can explain how something like photosynthesis works, yet it's at a loss explaining *why* there's life that requires photosynthesis to begin with.

So while I'm certain that the tsetse fly's reproductive habits might be unbelievably fascinating to an entomologist, those findings can be somewhat less satisfying to those existentially interested head-scratchers asking *why?*

That's where philosophy comes in. Philosophy explores the answers to what Russell called the "insoluble problems"—those important, yet seemingly impossible-to-solve existential and cosmological why questions related to not only the universe, but also our role and purpose within that universe.

Where philosophy differs from religion—because, as we've discussed, religion does presume to have the why questions all figured out—is that philosophy shies away from the self-assured superstition and dogma of religion; instead, philosophy attempts to discover the answer to those eternal questions via rational inquiry and contemplative effort.

But rational inquiry and contemplative philosophical meditation in ancient Greece were also inextricably enmeshed with cultural customs and theological beliefs (in the case of the metaphysical philosophers, with notions of what were variously called God, the Unmoved Mover, the One, and/or the Good), as well as in beliefs in a metaphysical (beyond-physical) Ideal Realm or Ideal Forms.

That's a critically important concept to keep in mind: for the ancient Greeks, philosophy, science, and religion weren't separate things—at least not in the sense where they were perceived as opposing perspectives. Instead, philosophy, science, and religion

How Plato and Pythagoras Can Save Your Life

were all integrated, complementary lenses that people had used to better understand and experience their world. Now, that's not to reductively say that philosophy, science, and religion were all the *same* thing, because there were important distinctions to be made between those various complementary lenses, but they weren't viewed as opposing ideologies, as they are today.

What that means for our chicken-crossing-the-road parable is that the ancient Greeks would have used all of those tools to better understand the chicken quest; they would have used science to understand the mechanics of the chicken's journey, they would have used philosophy to try and determine the purpose behind the road crossing, and, finally, they would have consulted with oracles or mystic sages to intuit the divine dimension of the chicken's traverse.

In addition to this integral approach, there's also one other very important distinction between ancient Greek philosophy and modern conceptions of philosophy.

When a historian like Bertrand Russell discusses and defines *philosophy*, he's really explicating what classical scholar and author Algis Uzdavinys calls philosophical *discourse*. That's very different from the Greek notion of philosophy being a lived *practice* instead of just an intellectual discussion. As Uzdavinys distinguishes in his important book *The Golden Chain: An Anthology of Pythagorean and Platonic Philosophy* (2004), discourse is analogous to theory (the Greek *Theoria*) and correlates more to later Occidental (European) notions of philosophy, while the essence of ancient Pythagorean and Platonic philosophy was *Praxis* (from the Greek root "to do") and meant the actual, lived application of philosophy—not just *talk* of philosophy.

In other words—and I'm sorry to use this cliché, but it needs to be said—the ancient Greeks walked the walk and didn't just talk the talk of philosophy; for them, philosophy was their way of life. I challenge you to find a philosophy professor today who can say the same thing.

But why is living a life informed by philosophy important? How can that be helpful to a person? And why do we, as humans, seem to *need* to better understand things, whether through religious practice, philosophical exploration, or the lens of science? Why is that we seem to *need* to know?

6

Homo Anxious:
I Think, Therefore I Worry

Why are humans the only primates that have developed religion? Why does philosopher Will Herberg call us "Homo Religiosus," a species that seems to need faith as much as it needs food or water? And why are we also the only species that has developed both philosophical systems and scientific methods of exploration?

Answer: Because we're so smart that we're scared out of our wits.

How's that? Well, our use of tools, a product of our handy-dandy opposable thumbs, allowed our brains (and our frontal lobes) to rapidly evolve and grow to the point where we were able to lift our heads up out of the dirt and the grind of survival long enough to be able to look up towards the starry sky and wonder. And while the ability to wonder and reflect is indeed a wonderful thing, it does, however, come at a price: it has made us nervous and anxious wrecks.

Allow me to explain.

The nature of existence and the infinite and uncharted universe—in all of its terrifying and unknown vastness—are rather daunting things to consider. Fortunately and, some might say, unfortunately, our evolved minds are, at least on this planet, uniquely able to apprehend and consider just how expansive that unknown universe might be. And that mysterious, unknown expanse simply scares the hell out of us.

And it's not just cosmological reflection that we find daunting. There's one other thing that our large brains are uniquely capable of (as far as we know), and that's also contributed to our emotional discomfort: our powerful intellects can apprehend the temporal notion of both past and future. While it may be true that being able to reflect on the past can help us to learn from our mistakes and that looking ahead into the future can help us to plan for that much-feared rainy day, there are also some negatives associated with this magical time-travelling ability.

In very broad strokes, there are several negative emotional states that are the outgrowths of our backwards and forward-looking ability: we can feel shame and guilt when regarding past conduct and events, and we can feel anxious and fearful when thinking about the unknown future—*especially* when thinking of our inevitable death. In other words, we're so smart, that, unlike members of the animal kingdom, who are living in happy, ignorant bliss about their impending mortality and their unknown futures, we *know* that death is gonna come-a-knockin'—and that terrifies us.

Indeed, Pulitzer Prize–winning author Ernest Becker had written in his seminal work *The Denial of Death* (1972) that, in essence, the sum of all of human endeavor—our art, our architecture, our religions, our procreation—are all just desperate attempts to deny our own mortality, to placate our terror (what psychologists call *Thanatos Anxiety*) over the possibility that there's nothing more beyond the physical realm.

And it's not just death that was scary; *life* could be pretty frightening as well—especially the mysterious and unknown dangers that were associated with the daily rigors of primitive

How Plato and Pythagoras Can Save Your Life

survival. When the original anthropoid—let's call him Caveman Bob—was first able to look out over the plains and consciously become aware of the predatory dangers that lurked in the high grasses—well, let's just say that was also probably the first time that a human developed an ulcer. It's not that gazelles don't instinctively know that tigers are bad and that dangers lurk; it's just that gazelles' brains don't allow them to ruminate and obsess over these things because, unlike us, they live in the moment. Unfortunately, as a byproduct of our powerful mind's ability to apprehend past and future (and, as mentioned, the accompanying guilt, fear, and anxiety that accompanies those thoughts), that simple way of being—the ability to be present in the here and now—is something many humans have lost. As a consequence, we, as a species, have become a nervous, anxious, self-medicating mess.

Yet some have realized the damage caused by ruminating and not living in the moment. Understanding the psychological and spiritual importance of being present, entire Buddhist belief systems, as well as various types of mindfulness-meditation techniques—not to mention the best-selling *The Power of Now* by Eckhart Tolle—were all developed to help us reconnect with that long-lost vestigial skill: our ability to experience the peace of the present moment.

Take a moment—no pun intended—to think about that: We gradually stopped living in the moment once our brains were able to conceptualize the concept of tomorrow, which then led to "What the hell else should I be worrying about for tomorrow? What else can eat me? How else can I die? What else can go wrong?!"

No wonder Caveman Bob was stressed out. Hell, you and I are stressed out, and we don't even have to worry about whose lunch we might be. We just have bills to pay, children to raise, jobs to maintain, relationships to handle. But at least all those issues are things that we kind of understand (well, except maybe the relationships part).

During Caveman Bob's time, not only did he have to worry about not being eaten, but he also lived in a world that was incomprehensible to him. Think about it: in prehistoric times, little of the natural world was understood. We tend to take for granted the comfort of a world that's been thoroughly deconstructed and demystified by the lens of science, but take a moment to try and appreciate what it might have been like during the dawn of humanity, when every strange bump in the night represented unknown mystery and danger. Today our young children sometimes cry at night for Mommy when they think there's a bogeyman under the bed, or if they think that a strange creaking in the closet might be a monster. But whom did Caveman Bob turn to when he saw and heard strange and scary things in the darkness? And how did he make sense of these unknown dangers?

Using the creative power of the human psyche, imaginative stories and myths were created to help early humans to understand their world; thus, every predator became a demon, every shadow a monster, every natural disaster the wrath of an angry deity, until eventually all of those interpretations of the natural world were woven into a cohesive and explanatory tale that tied into a creation myth.

The reason for this tendency towards story and myth is our *need* to make sense of our natural world; indeed, modern neuroscience research indicates that we're hard wired with this yearning to make sense of things. We even sometimes try and connect dots when those dots aren't actually connected. (See Chapter 8 and the discussion of optical illusions.) Thus, our brain will see a pattern that helps us to make sense of the nonsensical; that's why we see shapes in clouds or a man's face on the moon or conspiracies around every corner.

Those connections help create the illusion of order in the universe because we don't like randomness. In fact, psychologically, we need the comfort of order; it soothes us like a mother's embrace and makes us feel that the world is less threatening and that everything will be all right. Order, in its defeat over chaos, allows for the belief that there is, in fact, some sort of unifying purpose to help us make sense of our seemingly random universe.

It's with this quest to make sense of things—this need for order and purpose—that religion, science, and philosophy come in. They give us interpretive and explanatory frameworks for a better understanding of our world. They allow us to organize and process those overwhelming and sometimes frightening realities that our powerful minds are able to not only grasp, but, unfortunately, ruminate over as well.

While science tends to parse and deconstruct the minutiae of the natural world, religion and philosophy tackles the big questions head on. Whether these religious or philosophical frameworks are objectively valid lenses is irrelevant to the critically essential psychological role that they play in our emotional well-being. Valid or not, they act as soothing coping mechanisms (to use psychotherapeutic parlance) that help us deal with our "life is scary and overwhelming—and then you die" anxiety.

But religion and philosophy soothe us in very different ways.

Religion soothes our anxiety via the aforementioned explanatory stories and creation myths. These stories and myths help us understand how things came to be and how we should conduct ourselves (thus serving an important function by promoting a species-preserving social conformity). But they also help us understand how we might be able to get around that little thing called death, which seems to paralyze us with fear.

And that fear of death is a big-ticket item. It's why religion, like McDonald's, has served "billions and billions." Religion offers us a way to cheat death, because it promises spiritual immortality in the great hereafter, giving us a "get out of jail free" card that allows us to effectively bypass our date with the Grim Reaper. In that sense, religion is indeed a coping mechanism of the highest order—on both a personal and societal level—that helps us deal with our overwhelming Thanatos Anxiety. And, sure enough, there's been extensive research indicating that people who have some sort of faith or religion are actually healthier and happier and live longer lives—as well as die easier deaths—than those without. Indeed, there's ample literature in which hospice workers describe how people of faith die more peacefully than those without a belief system, who oftentimes have a look of anxious terror when they pass.

But does the research that illustrates the positive psychological benefit of religion in a person's life somehow refute the theological tenets of that religious system? Does, as many skeptics and atheists assert, the simple fact that a religious or spiritual belief acts as a soothing analgesic somehow prove that those spiritual beliefs are false? Does our psychological need for something preclude the existence of that something? Does, for example, a child's need for a mother's love preclude the existence of that mother's love?

I don't think so. In a later chapter, I'll address this very important notion that simply because something replete with fanciful mythology serves a soothing psychological purpose (Karl Marx once famously described religion as "the opium of the people"), that fact, in and of itself, does not preclude or refute the theological premises put forth by that belief system. Instead, it merely explains the psycho-social constructs and dynamics that often accompany such spiritual phenomena.

Some have suggested that religion, in addition to acting as a feel-good quasi-opiate, may also serve a rather Darwinian purpose as well. In Nicholas Wade's book *The Faith Instinct* (2009), the award-winning science writer for the *New York Times* rigorously

How Plato and Pythagoras Can Save Your Life

cites scientific evidence indicating that humans are hardwired to believe in the transcendent and further argues that our very survival required this belief. Wade takes the position that the evolution of man depended not only on individual natural selection, but also on the natural selection of groups. Since, the reasoning goes, religious doctrine imposes moral norms that facilitate collective survival in the name of a larger cause, groups held together by religion were more likely to survive than less-cohesive, nonreligious tribes. And since the socially more cohesive religious groups were more apt to survive, this religious tendency was passed down as a hereditary trait.

Molecular biologist Dean Hamer takes this genetic interpretation of religious experience one step further. In his controversial book *The God Gene* (2004), he not only claims that spirituality is an adaptive trait, but also claims to have actually located one of the genes responsible for that trait. This reduction of the spiritual experience to a physiological correlate was also claimed by several neuroscientists, who claimed to have found the "God spot" in our brain, the place where religious/ecstatic experiences were thought to be localized. However, more recent brain-imaging research seems to indicate that a variety of neural centers are actually involved and activated during spiritual or religious experiences.

Hamer's quest to localize and reduce spirituality to a gene began back in 1998, when he was conducting a survey on smoking and addiction for the National Cancer Institute. He had recruited over a thousand men and women, who agreed to take a standardized, 240-question personality test called the Temperament and Character Inventory (TCI). Among the many traits measured by the TCI was one called *self-transcendence*, which, in turn, consisted of three other sub-traits: *self-forgetfulness*, defined as the ability to get entirely lost in an experience; *transpersonal identification*, which is a feeling of connectedness to a larger universe; and *mysticism*, defined (quite problematically, in my opinion) as "an openness to things not literally provable." When all of these sub-traits were put together and scored, one was able to measure what would seem a rather difficult thing to quantify: a person's level of spirituality.

Hamer, resourceful devil that he is, gathered all of the data that had been collected for his smoking and addiction survey and decided to conduct a little spirituality study on the side. He went about ranking all the participants along the self-transcendence scale of the TCI, placing them on a continuum from least to most spiritually inclined.

Then he went gene hunting. He wanted to see if there was any correlation between being spiritual and the presence or absence of any corresponding gene. This was no easy trick, since the human genome contains 35,000 genes consisting of 3.2 billion chemical bases. To narrow his search, Hamer focused in on nine specific genes known to play major roles in the production of brain chemicals known as monoamines—which include serotonin, norepinephrine, and dopamine—which regulate such essential functions as mood and motor control.

After studying the genetic samples that his subjects provided, he hit pay dirt. He discovered that a variation in a gene known as VMAT2 seemed to directly correlate to how the volunteers had scored on the self-transcendence scale. Those with the nucleic acid cytosine in one particular spot on the VMAT2 gene ranked high, while those with the nucleic acid adenine in the same spot ranked lower.

Hamer had done it. He had successfully reduced spirituality to a microscopic speck on an otherwise unremarkable gene. The tendency to seek God—to transcend, to experience union with the infinite cosmos—was all reduced to the positioning of a tiny little nucleic acid.

So that's it spiritual seekers; pack up your tents and call it a day. Nothing else to see here. The riddle of God has been solved! And all it took was a rather clever molecular biologist to sort it all out!

But did he?

Hamer is what one might call a scientific reductionist or a scientific materialist; he's one of those scientists that I spoke about earlier who likes to deconstruct and reduce a phenomenon down into tiny, quantifiable bits without considering that the phenomenon they're exploring may synergistically be more than just the sum of its various parts. But that doesn't seem to register for reductionists/deconstructionists. In a *Time* magazine cover story (October 25, 2004) entitled "The God Gene," Hamer expressed his view on what it means to be human: "I'm a believer that every thought that we think and every feeling that we feel is the result of activity in the brain. I think we follow the basic law of nature, which is that we're a bunch of chemical reactions running around in a bag."

How very special. Human beings as nothing more than chemical reactions running around in a bag! What a visionary and uplifting sentiment of the human potential given by our Dr. Hamer!

That's what scientific reductionists do; they break things down until they're no longer recognizable. So they reduce the human condition down to approximately nine dollars worth of chemicals, wrapped and shaken in skin and served refreshingly at 98.6 degrees Fahrenheit. And that's it—that's the sum whole of what we are.

Our soul, or to use more secular language, our *consciousness*, we are told by these enlightened neuroscientists, is merely an "epiphenomenon" of our brains—that is to say, dependent on and a byproduct of said brain. Pull the plug on our heart—the brain's biological battery—and the screen fades to black. No brain activity, no consciousness. No consciousness, definitely no soul.

As I've mentioned, a major problem with the deconstructive reductionism of most materialist scientists is the failure to recognize that most phenomena work synergistically to be more than the sum of their parts, just as wood, violin strings, and a musician's trained fingertips can converge together in a perfect storm of brilliance to create a Vivaldi violin concerto that is much more than just the wood and string of the violin randomly shaken, and just as nine dollars' worth of chemicals become much more than "chemicals running around in a bag" when animated by the life force. While studying those various chemical elements that come together to create a human being might lead to some interesting chemistry insights, those efforts will reveal nothing of the synergistic phenomenon that those chemicals (with a little animating, Dr. Frankenstein–like jolt of electricity) come together to create: a human being. Studying sulfur or magnesium will tell you absolutely nothing about love, or the thirst to create, or our ability to write epic poetry or compose breath-taking music. It will yield no insights into our ability to imagine (and sometimes perceive) infinite worlds and infinite levels of realities.

No, studying magnesium won't illuminate the larger human process, and studying genes does not reveal the full spiritual picture. Sorry, Dr. Hamer.

I somewhat facetiously mentioned the animating jolt of electricity as being the thing that makes us come alive, but what about this thing called a soul, the animating force that René Descartes had viewed as the "ghost in the machine"? Where in Hamer's bag of chemicals is the soul?

Now, I fully understand that talk of a soul brings smug snickering from the scientific materialists who think that we shouldn't waste time and research on such an unscientific (meaning, we can't readily *observe* it) concept. But to them I would say, "Not so fast." There does indeed seem to be quite a bit of research indicating that our *consciousness* (the secular term that I'll use instead of *soul*) can exist beyond just our biological brain; research that would seem to suggest that, in fact, consciousness is more than just the epiphenomenon of the brain that neuroscientists insist it is. Indeed, there have been rigorous, repeatable, and statistically significant consciousness studies done by researchers like Dean Radin and my friend and mentor William Braud that point to consciousness having an effect beyond just its neurobiological domain. This profound research indicates that the invisible hands of consciousness are somehow able to interact with the physical world and that there is indeed an entire universe of unseen realities.

Perhaps, as some have theorized, the reason that thoughts and matter can interact is because they are essentially different manifestations of the same thing. Albert Einstein established that matter is really compact and dense energy; in the same way, perhaps consciousness, in the form of thoughts, is composed of the same elemental stuff as matter (perhaps the tiny subatomic filaments of string theory, albeit unseen by our technology) and is, in fact, merely a different manifestation or variation of a larger continuum.

This theory defies the post–Newtonian-Cartesian paradigms, which seem to tell us that if we can't see or measure something, it can't exist—and that includes God, the human soul, cosmic consciousness, the collective unconscious, or any kind of spiritual (i.e., non-corporeal) dimension. But even though we can't see gravity (or fully understand it, for that matter), we acknowledge that it exists. Even though we can't see the source that the great artistic masters draw their creative inspiration from, their paintings most certainly exist. And what of love? And ideas? They're all invisible phenomena, yet are they not real?

Sure, the most cynical and reductionist of the neuroscientists may tell us that all these phenomena (except for the external and collectively experienced gravity) are all interior neuroprocesses—neurons and synapses firing to create the illusion of external phenomena. They may explain that love is only a conditioned and learned neural-feedback loop. Ideas and dreams? More neurochemistry, nothing more.

But if consciousness research indicates that there is more to who we are than synapses and neurons, perhaps the neuroscientists have deconstructed only the mechanism that helps us actualize consciousness—*not* consciousness's source.

The analogy here is an old transistor radio or cathode-tube TV. When the TV or radio is plugged in (when their "heart" is active), they come "alive" to produce music or screen images. What is the source of the radio's music or of the TV's picture? When we become like the neuroscientist and attempt to deconstruct them, we think we have it figured out. Aha! There is no source, we think; the music and the picture are all just epiphenomena of the TV or radio hardware.

But the "soul" of that radio or TV really exists in an invisible plane—the airwaves. This invisible plane, which we cannot see, hear, or touch, is the causal source that animates the radio or TV and makes it come alive (after it's been plugged in). The cathode tubes and transistors, like so many neurons and brain hemispheres, are the necessary mechanisms to actualize the *process* of the life of both the radio and the TV, but they ain't the source.

We can't see the airwaves, just as we can't see the causal informational realm that Plato and Pythagoras believed existed, just as we can't see the strings of superstring theory, just as we can't (usually) see Ultimate Reality, or God, for that matter. And since we can't see all those things, the empirical sciences would have us shut the door on even allowing for the possibility of those unseen realities. Just as the high priests of science would, if not entirely denounce a spiritual experience, most certainly reduce it to a gene variation or a soothing fiction created by a psychologically needy mind.

Religion as an opiate, religion via natural selection as an inherited gene, religion as a way to help us make sense of the world—as I asked earlier, do all of these explanations and deconstructions of the religious (or spiritual) experience preclude the existence of a God?

The question that really begs asking is, which came first, God or the need for God?

Some have argued that perhaps the neuropsychological need or tendency to seek God has been hardwired into us by that very same transcendent intelligence. Sort of like the homing pigeon seeks the home it was trained to find, humans may be seeking what they were programmed to seek. And gene VMAT2 can help facilitate that process, just as religion can help facilitate that spiritual journey home.

In my experience, when discussing religion with intelligent non-religious people, they often exhibit a visible discomfort with the mention of the word *God*. Perhaps, in addition to the baggage that organized religion has brought upon itself, there is also a semantic problem with regard to how people define God.

Without getting caught up in the cultural and religious projections of an anthropomorphic God that looks like Moses and carries a big staff, what if we consider the idea that perhaps God is merely the universe made sentient by our sentience; perhaps if "I think, therefore I am" is true, then the universe, through us, its sentient beings, also thinks and therefore is.

The analogy here is neurons in a brain. The neuron is an individual living cell, yet it comes together with billions of other living cells to become a part of the larger consciousness of the brain. Is it possible, that *we* are the neurons in the mind of God? (Feel free to substitute the word *universe* for *God* if the G word has too much baggage for you.)

Just a thought.

Admittedly, all of the research regarding our hardwired tendency to seek transcendence does nothing to either prove or disprove the existence of God or any other sort of spiritual or metaphysical reality; it merely helps to explain the human tendency towards spiritual experience a bit better.

Unfortunately, it would seem that finding scientific proof of God or any other kinds of transcendent realities can be a rather tricky thing. And it's this matter of proof and evidence that gets to the source of the modern conflict between science and religion: science demands affirmative proof for what is essentially unprovable in the scientific arena. But, as we'll see in the next chapter, perhaps when it comes to matters of "proof" regarding the existence of God, maybe the evidentiary burden should instead fall on the atheists to prove that there is not a God or, at the very least, that there isn't some sort of cosmic purpose; indeed, if atheists are so quick to invoke science as their guiding rationale towards the belief in a random universe without a God, then they should—as science requires—prove it. Because, contrary to popular opinion, the other side of the God debate has indeed provided some proof; as we'll soon see, using the laws of logic, a wise philosopher during the Middle Ages actually did provide what has become known as a "proof for God."

7

Newsflash: Science Declares God Is Dead—But Can't Prove It!

(or The Scientific Atheism Fallacy)

A scientist *has* to be an atheist; that seems to be the pervading wisdom put forth by a smug intelligentsia. Yahoos, snake handlers, and Bible freaks are "true believers," but sober men and women of science can't possibly believe in such fairy tales. Snicker, snicker, wink, wink. If you're smart, then obviously you get that God is a convenient psychological crutch and religion nothing more than a social mechanism designed to reign in our baser tendencies—tendencies that, if uncontrolled by the dos and don'ts of religion would lead to societal anarchy.

This idea that atheism is the ideology of choice for the more educated and enlightened and can be the only mind-set of the rational and scientifically minded (since, you know, there's no scientific proof of God) is championed in best sellers such as Christopher Hitchens' *God Is Not Great* (2007) and Richard Dawkins' *The God Delusion* (2006). So-called smart people—you know, academics, scientists, intellectuals, and wannabe intellectuals—declare themselves atheists with a capital A and tow the company line: since God, or cosmic sentience, can't be affirmatively proven (or even observed) via scientific methodology, then those empirically unobservable things can't exist. Thus, anything beyond our observable material reality is considered right up there with Big Foot and the chupacabra.

But here's the thing. If any scientists proudly and self-assuredly declare themselves atheists (Richard Dawkins and friends, you know who you are!), then they're not only being intellectually dishonest, but they're also going counter to the guiding principles of the thing that they profess to love so much: science.

How's that?

In science, we can't affirmatively know something until we've empirically proven it. Absent any such affirmative data, the true and proper scientific stance should be one that echoes Socrates' credo "I know that I don't know." (Socrates is said to have been dubbed by the Oracle at Delphi the smartest man in all of Greece because he alone was smart enough to realize that "I know that I know nothing.") Thus, without any affirmative scientific proof that God *does not* exist, the default position should be one of agnosticism—of "I don't know since I don't have enough data one way or another." Really, how can Dawkins claim, as a scientist, that he's an atheist when he hasn't proven that God does not exist?

The atheist will counter by crying, "Well, OK, but there isn't any affirmative proof *of* God." Fine, even if we grant that assertion (which some will dispute), then the proper scientific stance should still be one of uncertain agnosticism—not definitive atheism. Indeed, one might argue that skeptical agnosticism is the orientation consistent with science, pending any affirmative proof of God's existence one way or the other.

Now, some might echo the old axiom that, well, you *can't* prove a negative. But if we were to believe that, then that's all the more reason why a person of science should not claim to be an

How Plato and Pythagoras Can Save Your Life

atheist since *the nonexistence of God is* empirically impossible to prove. Many have disputed this old "you can't prove a negative" axiom by pointing out that some scientific experiments do indeed prove a negative; Francesco Redi's famous seventeenth-century experiment proving that maggots *do not* spontaneously generate from meat is an example of proving a negative). Yet where is the experiment to show that God does not exist or the proof that the universe has no purpose? Absent these, it would seem that for a scientist to embrace atheism is not only intellectually dishonest, but also logically inconsistent.

One might also reasonably say that theistically inclined scientists are also guilty of intellectual dishonesty; after all, they too believe in something that hasn't been scientifically proven, which, as we've said, is a big scientific no-no.

But *there is* a logically consistent proof for the existence of God. It's not commonly taught in most public schools, but Saint Thomas Aquinas, the thirteenth-century philosopher and theologian, developed his "five proofs for the existence of God" hundreds of years before an apple dropped on Isaac Newton's head. In essence, Aquinas argues that something (i.e., us, the universe) can't arise from nothingness, that something (namely God) had to be the cause of all things and of all movement. (This notion borrows heavily from Aristotle's "Unmoved Mover" conception of what we might call God.)

Aquinas's second key idea has to do with the universe's tendency towards order, which seems to contradict the chaos of the laws of entropy; in other words, the order that comes from disorder leads to a conclusion that the universe has some sort of purposeful unfolding (what some might call divine intervention or perhaps even a form of universal DNA encoded into the existential fabric to guide, over the course of some 15 billion years, the evolutionary development of an inanimate, subatomic, pre–Big Bang speck from inanimate star dust into the sentient and reasoned being that's reading this page).

To give a better explication of Aquinas's five proofs of the existence of God, I provide the following brief summary, from S. M. Miranda's website. at "St. Thomas Aquinas Forum" (*www.saintaquinas.com*; the bold is my addition).

Aquinas' **first proof** is through the argument of motion. It can be noted that some things in the universe are in motion and it follows that whatever is in the state of motion must have been placed in motion by another such act. Motion in itself is nothing less than the reduction of something from the state of potentiality to actuality. Because something can not be in potentiality and actuality simultaneously, it follows that something can not be a mover of itself. A simple example of this is a rubber ball motionless on a flat surface. It has the potential for motion, but is not currently in the state of actual motion. In order for this to happen, something else in motion must set the ball in motion, be that gravity, another moving object or the wind. And yet something must have set that object in motion as well (even gravity, a force caused by matter warping the space-time fabric, attributes its existence to pre-existing matter and the exchange of pre-existing graviton particles). Thus pre-existing motions cause all motions. Yet, this chain can not extend into infinity because that would deny a first mover that set all else in motion. Without a first mover, nothing could be set in motion. Thus we acknowledge the first and primary mover as God.

How Plato and Pythagoras Can Save Your Life

The **second proof** follows closely with the first and expounds the principle of causality. St. Thomas explains that in the world of sense there is an order of cause and effect. There is a cause for all things such as the existence of a clock. And nothing can cause itself into existence. A clock cannot will itself into existence, it must be created and caused into existence by something else. A clockmaker creates a clock and causes its existence, and yet the material of the clock and the clockmaker did not cause themselves to exist. Something else must have caused their existence. All things can attribute their existence to a first cause that began all causes and all things. We call this first cause God.

Aquinas **next** explains that things of this universe have a transitory nature in which they are generated and then corrupt over time. Because of this the things of nature can be said to be "possible to be and possible not to be." Since it is impossible for these things always to exist, then it indicates a time when they did not exist. If there are things which are transitory (and are possible not to be) then at one time there could have been nothing in existence. However, as was already explained in his second proof, there must have been a first cause that was not of transitory nature that could have generated the beginning of nature.

In his **fourth point** Aquinas notes that there is a certain gradation in all things. For instance we can group things that are hot according to varying degrees of the amount of heat perceptible in that object. In classifying objects there is always something which displays the maximum fullness of that characteristic. Thus universal qualities in man such as justice and goodness must attribute their varying qualities to God; the source of maximum and perfect justice and goodness.

Finally, Thomas Aquinas says that the order of nature presupposes a higher plan in creation. The laws governing the universe presuppose a universal legislature who authored the order of the universe. We cannot say that chance creates order in the universe. If you drop a cup on the floor it shatters into bits and has become disordered. But if you were to drop bits of the cup, they would not assemble together into a cup. This is an example of the inherent disorder prevalent in the universe when things are left to chance. The existence of order and natural laws presupposes a divine intelligence who authored the universe into being.

Now, Aquinas's proof relies on reason and logic; for those seeking C.S.I.-style evidence of God, sorry. Nor do we have the George Burns version of God from the movie *Oh, God!* testifying in a courtroom or revealing himself to a befuddled John Denver.

Instead, all we have is a thirteenth-century proof from a long-dead theologian. That and wondrous and miraculous creation itself—flowers, and babies, and rainbows, and luminous stars and galaxies, and, perhaps most amazing of all, this amazing thing called the human mind with its seemingly infinite ability to create and to imagine. Yes, this incredible mind of ours that bestows—or receives—sentience that then allows us to look up at the brilliance of the night sky and wonder.

Even though everything that I've just mentioned might not convince everyone that there's more to the universe than meets the eye, I have still yet to see the compelling proof or the scientific evidence that God or cosmic purpose *does not* exist. So for all of you atheists out there, be *really* smart: Admit that you don't know for sure what the hell is going on. Be like our man Socrates and admit that you know that you don't know. After all, for all you *really* know, you might just be a butterfly dreaming that you're an atheist!

With all of this talk of God, atheism, and science, we come back around to philosophy, the thing that Bertrand Russell had described as "the no-man's land between religion and science." Where does philosophy fit in to all of this discussion about God, science, and what it means to be human?

Exercise 4

Mindfulness Walk: Being Without Thinking

This contemplative exercise involves trying to stop all our left-hemisphere-mind verbal chatter and the inner self-talk that we call thinking.

For this exercise, you will take a fifteen- to twenty-minute walk somewhere in nature. However, this is a very special type of walk; **you will be asked to not verbally think during this walk.** When verbal chatter arises in your consciousness, gently push it away. For this walk, **you will be asked to immerse yourself into your surroundings,** to become keenly aware of all the subtleties and details of the nature that you will be walking through.

Thus, **as you *very slowly* walk along,** be observant and **aware of the colors and texture** of the tree, the **feel of the ground under each step,** the sensation of the fresh air as you inhale it through your nostrils, the vivid color kaleidoscope of natural colors along your path. As thoughts and words arise, continue to gently push them away.

At the end of the fifteen or twenty minutes, **find a tree, rock, plant, or shrub to stand in front of.** As you stand in front of this fellow living creature, become keenly aware of all its textural nuances and details. **Begin to experience this tree (if you've chosen a tree) to be a fellow living object. Feel your life force—what the Japanese call your Ki—going down through your legs and into the ground**; this life force is anchoring you into Gaia, Mother Earth, just as the tree's roots are anchoring it into the ground. Take several moments to merely *be* with the tree. Do you feel your Ki touching the tree's roots? If not, **take several more moments to visualize your Ki-roots and the tree's actual roots connecting with each other through the living earth beneath your feet.**

When you're done, sit for several more moments and become aware of how you feel. Now look around you; do you experience things any differently? **Feel free to write down any of these initial thoughts and feelings,** as writing these down will help you to process this experience.

How Plato and Pythagoras Can Save Your Life

8

Why Philosophy Matters

If philosophy asks the *why* questions, perhaps it's appropriate for us to ask *why* philosophy? Why live life embracing the contemplation of the so-called insoluble problems of existence? And why use *philosophia* as the guiding light that informs and shapes our very being? After all, if the problems contemplated are indeed unknowable and insoluble, then what's the point?

Well, there are a couple of reasons why philosophy matters. The first and most superficial reason is that, like religion, philosophy helps us to better understand our world and make sense of things. But unlike religion, which relies on faith and doctrine, discursive philosophy teaches us how to use our reasoning minds to reach our own conclusions about the nature of the universe and our purpose within that larger reality. And by better understanding ourselves and our universe, we can attempt to reconcile whether or not there's a method to the madness—whether, in fact, there may be a purpose to things.

Our old friend Bertrand Russell discussed the notion of exploring this cosmic purpose as a key reason for the embrace of philosophy. Russell explained that in our quest for cosmic purpose, we might also ameliorate what he called the "terror of cosmic loneliness." (There's that damned anxiety thing again! I must admit, I often wonder if a horse effortlessly racing through a field experiences the terror of cosmic loneliness.)

What is cosmic purpose? It's the belief that the universe isn't random, that evolution indeed has a purpose. However, whether or not we ascribe theological dimensions to this non-randomness is, according to Russell, entirely optional. That's because, as he describes it, the "doctrine" of cosmic purpose can have three forms: theistic (God controls the universe, and our purpose is God-driven); pantheistic (God *is* the universe, and it's unfolding in accordance with some larger plan); and, finally, emergent (universal purpose is less obvious and emerges rather blindly from one stage to the next). This third form is more of a secular, DNA-style of universal unfolding.

If we chose to reject all of the above three suppositions, then the default option is that the universe is purposeless, that our lives are random and part of a larger consortium of yet more random processes without any sort of designed *telos* (Greek for "end"). But how do those who conceptualize their lives as a random process within yet a larger random process experience their world and conduct their lives? Conversely, how do people who embrace some sense of purpose-driven evolutionary unfolding navigate through their world? Answer: Very differently.

And this brings us to yet another reason why philosophy is relevant. It's the notion that the way that we understand our world—the way that we conceptualize our worldview—in turn, shapes the way that we live our lives; in other words, the way we think influences the way we live. And the converse is also true: the way we live influences the way we think. As Russell puts it: "There is a reciprocal causation: the circumstances of men's lives do much to determine their philosophy, but, conversely, their philosophy does much to determine their circumstances."

And, sure enough, we have centuries of history to bear this out. There are countless examples where we can say that socioeconomic circumstances impacted the belief system a person adopted, as well as the converse, that a person's belief system impacted the many variable factors in that person's life. So a person's philosophical orientation (admittedly shaped by his or her circumstances) will go a long way in determining the trajectory of one's life. We'd expect an anarchist to live a different sort of life than an Orthodox Jew; atheists will experience their world differently than, say, Islamic fundamentalists.

Philosophy, then, can be important if for no other reason than it can shape a person's life by providing a lens that can help that person determine which worldview to embrace—and, in so doing—can change one's life course.

There's also one other reason to embrace philosophy—at least the *lived-practice* philosophy of ancient Greek metaphysics that we spoke about earlier in this chapter. This final reason can, in my estimation, be the most essential reason of all to embrace philosophy: by *living* philosophy as a mind-body-spirit purification, as the original philosophers like Pythagoras had conceived, we can experience an alchemical transformation—the Greek miracle—and thus become attuned to our higher cosmic purpose.

This book is an explication of that attunement. Part III will explore and explain some of the fundamental ideas and precepts that informed this type of transformative Greek wisdom. What we'll discover is that the ancient Greeks were *very* interested in the true nature of reality.

Exercise 5

Am I a Neuron in the Mind of God?

This contemplative exercise deals with **how we experience ourselves within the larger universal reality.** Philosophy, it has been said, is a pursuit of cosmological and ontological truth. In the first contemplative exercise, we asked ourselves, who—and what—are we? It is time to ask those questions yet again.

But before we begin, **take a few minutes to do some sort of physical exercise,** being sure to only do as much as your physical health allows. This could include **walking, jogging, or bicycling.** After **fifteen to thirty minutes** (depending on your health) of exercise, **find a body of water to sit facing in quiet contemplation.** This can be a pond, a river, a lake, or a pool. If there are no appropriate bodies of water, light a candle and meditate while focusing on the flickering flame.

Now ask yourself the question, in light of the readings in this previous chapter, **who—and what—am I?** As you ask it, allow your consciousness to be absorbed by the water in front of you; **feel yourself merge into the liquid.** As you merge into the oceanic state, **become aware of the cells within your body and, more specifically, the neurons—by some estimates over 100 billion—in your mind.** Are they alive as discrete living creatures? **Are you aware of how their individual and biological functions contribute to your survival as you sit contemplating the water?** Ask yourself again, what am I?

Finally, ask yourself this question: am I a neuron in the mind of God? (Or feel free to use the more secular term *universe.*) Take several minutes to allow the universe to respond.

When you're done, sit for several more moments and become aware of how you feel. Now look around you; do you experience things any differently? **Feel free to write down any of these initial thoughts and feelings,** as writing these down will help you to process this experience.

PART THREE

Reality Bites

The world of things we perceive is but a veil.
—Abraham J. Heschel

There are things known and there are things unknown,
and in between are the doors of perception.
—Aldous Huxley

9

The Physical World:
The Tip of the Reality Iceberg

Do you believe the old adage "seeing is believing"? Are you like our friends from Missouri, the "Show Me State," where seeing something is the equivalent of confirming that it exists?

If you do think that seeing is indeed believing, then ask yourself, is this always true? Are our eyes the most reliable means of discerning reality? Or, for that matter, are any of our senses really reliable when it comes to perceiving what's real?

Well, I can say this: Plato and Pythagoras sure didn't think so.

Just ask yourself, have your eyes ever played tricks on you? Have you ever thought that you saw something, but then realized maybe you hadn't really seen what you thought you had seen?

For instance, have you ever been driving late at night on a long, repetitive stretch of highway when all of a sudden you could have sworn that you saw something—perhaps a shadow—on the road? But then, after rubbing your weary eyes a bit, you realized that it was just a road gremlin? Road gremlins are the highway versions of the airborne gremlins that fatigued fighter pilots during World War II were convinced that they had seen mischievously wrecking havoc on the their engines while in flight. (*Twilight Zone* fans will remember the classic episode "Terror at 20,000 Feet," in which a young and ruddy faced William Shatner played the role of a wild-eyed and hallucinating—or was he?—airplane passenger that keeps seeing a hairy gremlin doing a tap-tap-tap number on the engine immediately outside of his window.)

And what about optical illusions? We've all seen the ones where one line looks shorter than the other, but is actually the same length as the other. This was an optical illusion first developed by Italian psychologist Mario Ponzo (see figures 3 and 4). It demonstrated the mind's ability to subjectively judge an object's size based on its background.

Our pattern-seeking brains often see what's not there: Aoccdring to rscheearch at Cmabbrigde Uinervtisy, it deosn't mttaer in what order the ltteers in a word are, the only iprmoatnt thing is that the frist and lsat ltteer be in the rghit pclae. The rset can be a taotl mses and you can sitll raed it wouthit a porbelm.

Were you able to read the preceding passage? If you were, then your mind was "seeing" and reading what really wasn't there. Your brain was interpreting the letters in a way that makes sense for it; it read an actual word even when the word was spelled out very differently than it should have been.

Then there are the more dramatic natural optical illusions like sunsets and rainbows. Is the sun actually going down in the horizon? And is a rainbow *really* there, or does it merely exist in the visual cortex of our brains as we process the refracting light?

For that matter, does *any* color really exist, in the objective phenomenological sense? Is a brown chair really brown? Or is the color that we think that something is—the color that we see it as—merely, as scientists tell us, the color of the visible

How Plato and Pythagoras Can Save Your Life

spectrum that the object doesn't absorb and reflects back to us? Really, one can say that my brown chair is actually every color *except* brown.

Of course, any conversation about the *appearance* of color would have to mention that color is just a byproduct of our biological hardware and the way that we visually process things. So what would my chair look like if I were able to perceive and process a wider range of the radiation spectrum—say, infrared? Well, I can tell you that my chair would no longer look brown.

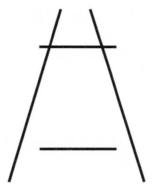

Figure 3. *The Ponzo optical illusion*

The Ponzo optical illusion was first demonstrated by the Italian psychologist Mario Ponzo (1882–1960) in 1913. He suggested that the human mind judges an object's size based on its background. The typical example of this hypothesis is the figure. The vertical lines appear to go off into the distance, like train tracks. This gives us the impression that the line in the distance is larger than the line that appears to be nearer to the viewer.

Figure 4. Photo illustration of the Ponzo optical illusion
This great photo presents the Ponzo optical illusion slightly differently.
The three horizontal lines are exactly the same length.

So the eyes can play tricks, and then the mind filters what the eyes "think" they see, and then our memory further filters and interprets that data. Hell, any fan of courtroom dramas or any beginning district attorney knows that eyewitness accounts are the least reliable form of evidence and, thus, not really great tools towards objective truth. And let's talk about hallucinations. Is a hallucination a byproduct of a neurochemical imbalance or, rather, of a more sensitized sensory system? Are people that see things that others don't simply crazy (to use a very politically incorrect term for mentally ill), or do they possess the sixth sense that the little kid who "sees dead people" in the 1999 film *The Sixth Sense* made so famous? As I like to say, one man's schizophrenic is another man's John Edward (of *Crossing Over* TV fame)—or saint, for that matter.

Almost ten years ago I had the opportunity to work with my first certifiably psychotic patient while interning at a psychiatric hospital as part of my graduate studies. There's nothing quite like working with an actively hallucinating schizophrenic; I'll never forget my encounter with this particularly intense man in his late thirties with piercing blue eyes who would claim to see archangels. He'd vividly describe hideous, fifteen-foot-tall, muscular and hoofed archangels that looked like "Satan's gargoyles" as his eyes would widen and sweat would pour down his terrified face.

This terrified look that so many schizophrenics seem to exhibit is an expression of what psychologists call existential terror. I mean, think about it: for an actively hallucinating schizophrenic, distinguishing between what's real and what's not real is no easy trick. You see things, sometimes hoofed and horrible, as clearly as you or I see the bus that takes us to work every morning. One could only imagine how truly terrifying that must be.

As mental-health clinicians, we tend to discount these apparent hallucinations as the mad rantings of a chemically imbalanced mind. Still, it would give me pause to think: am I really so sure that he's not seeing what he says he sees?

One particular morning, my archangel-seeing patient's visions were more vivid and intense than usual.

"They're everywhere—here in the hospital; these fifteen-foot monsters are all over the place!" he said very excitedly, as his blond hair started to stick to the beads of sweat on his forehead.

"But if they're fifteen feet tall, how do they fit in the hospital?" I naively asked.

With an exasperated tone, my schizophrenic charge yelled out, "They're bent over, at the waist! That's how they fit!" Then more quietly, he added, "But when they go outside in the parking lot, it's amazing. They slowly stand up and unfurl their wings. Shit, they're almost thirty feet across with their wingspan! But then when they fly away, they're wings don't move. It's as if they just float up. Don't you think that's odd?"

"Very. Do you see them now?" I asked.

"Yes."

"Where?"

With this question, he leaned in very close to me—so close that his nose almost touched mine. Hell, he was so close that I could smell the tuna lunch he'd eaten earlier on his breath. Those cobalt eyes danced as they pierced mine. Then he leaned back, and it became obvious that he was looking at something just over my shoulders.

I asked him again, "Where do you see them?"

A little half smile came over his face as he calmly and slowly answered, "There are two standing right behind you."

I'm not going to lie; every bone in my body was telling me to quickly turn around so that I might catch a glimpse of what he was seeing. But I didn't, even though I don't automatically discount unusual experiences immediately out of hand. Yes, sometimes such experiences are indicative of an underlying psychiatric disorder—perhaps a neurochemical imbalance, a little too much dopamine kicking around in the visual cortex, stimulating the brain to see what's not there.

But not always.

As I said, one man's schizophrenic is another man's saint—or person with paranormal abilities.

So whether it's the result of optical illusions, hallucinations, or just fatigue, our senses can sometimes deceive us.

But here's a very important point regarding the mistrust that the ancient Greek mystic philosophers had towards the senses: philosophers like Plato didn't merely believe that our senses were limited because they were sometimes faulty during hallucinations or optical illusions; these philosophers felt that even when our eyes were "accurately" seeing things, they *still* didn't perceive "true" reality because the physical, material world available to us via our senses wasn't the deeper level of fundamental reality. In fact, the material world was a mere shadow of this deeper level of reality (a.k.a., the Ideal Realm).

I need to also make another very important point. When discussing distinctions between the reality that we can see, hear, smell, and touch (the sensorial physical world) versus an unseen, transcendent reality that we've described as a deeper level of reality, people sometimes use semantic shortcuts that simplify that distinction as "illusory" versus "real" reality. But as a very wise doctoral student of mine at the Institute of Transpersonal Psychology would always point out, such labels should not negate or lessen the realness of the physical world. Calling the sensorial world an illusion is a bit of a misleading oversimplification that tends to privilege the transcendent. The physical world *is* real; it's just not all that there is.

A better analogy for the relationship between the physical and the metaphysical might be that of an iceberg. All that we can see—all that we can experience with our senses—is that 10 percent tip floating above the frigid waters, but there's much more to that iceberg that we can't see, lurking beneath the surface. (An unlucky captain of the *Titanic* found that out the hard way.) The illusion—the deception—occurs when we confuse the tip with the entire iceberg, or when we buy into the fallacy that our senses are revealing the whole reality ball of wax or, to keep my metaphors consistent, the whole iceberg.

There's similar semantic confusion in Hinduism with the definition of *Maya*. Very often, people use *Maya* as shorthand for the illusion of the physical world when, in fact, it's not the physical world that's the illusion; rather, the illusion is the *false belief* that the physical world is all that there is. Indeed, using *Maya* to mean just the illusory physical world is the mistake of confusing the tip for the entire iceberg.

Greek mystic philosophy was all about experiencing the entire iceberg. It was the method and means by which the human psyche (or soul) could get beyond the distortion of the senses and purify itself in order to experience—or actually *merge* with—this deeper (iceberg) level of reality in what's known as *mystical union*.

But the necessary first step of that process is embracing the notion that our senses are very, very limited in revealing reality in all of its paradoxical and unseen fullness.

So what side of the "seeing is believing" debate do you fall on? Just ask yourself these questions: Do you believe that everything that exists in the universe lends itself to empirical observation? Or, instead, are there things out there that are beyond our senses?

For the purposes of this book, our journey will take us into the realm of the mystic; like the Van Morrison song says, we're headed "Into the Mystic." And, like the ancient Greeks, we're taking a road that's not only beyond the senses but, as we'll read more about in the next chapter, is strangely beyond reason as well.

So buckle down and strap in as we journey out onto this magical, mystical, *transrational* highway.

How Plato and Pythagoras Can Save Your Life

Exercise 6

More to Reality Than Meets the Eye

This exercise deals with **reality and our senses.** Take the opportunity to sit in a chair in a room without any distractions (i.e., a room without any TV, computer, or music on). Sit in a relaxed and comfortable position, with both feet on the floor and your hands relaxed on top of your thighs; keep your posture straight and your eyes loosely focusing on a point several feet in front of you.

Begin to breathe in slowly through your nose and then out through your mouth. Gently try and still any turbulence that might be occurring in the ocean of your mind.

After several minutes of this relaxed breathing, **begin to become aware and to appreciate your senses, one by one.** Become aware of your sight; appreciate the colors and the shapes that you are seeing. Then focus on your hearing; what does the stillness sound like? Then observe your sense of smell; are there any odors that you're noticing? Then shift to your sense of touch; become aware of the chair as it holds you up, the floor under your feet. What other sensations are you feeling?

After becoming very aware of your senses, **begin to think about what you've just read in the preceding chapter about the senses and illusion.** Ask yourself this question: how accurate are your senses *really* in perceiving the essence of the room that you are sitting in? **What might the walls "look" like without the visible light spectrum?** What might any other object "look" like? **What might the room "look" like on a molecular and subatomic level?**

Finally, spend several minutes attempting to experience the room that you're in without benefit of your five senses.

When you're done, sit for several more moments and become aware of how you feel. Now look around you; do you experience things any differently? **Feel free to write down any of these initial thoughts and feelings,** as writing these down will help you to process this experience.

10

Real Deal Reality: Beyond Sense and Beyond Reason

"God is dead" Friedrich Nietzsche once famously said.

The nineteenth-century German philosopher wrote this God obituary in *The Gay Science* (a.k.a., *Joyous Wisdom)*, as he described an exchange between a lantern-yielding "madman" seeking God in a marketplace full of cynical atheists. While those gathered in the marketplace taunt the madman with laughter and jeers ("Is God hiding? Did he lose his way like a child?"), the madman responds, "Where has God gone? I shall tell you. We have killed him—you and I. We are his murderers."

And you know what else we've murdered, what else is dead in the modern age?

The human soul.

Alas, the subject of poets and romantics is done, kaput. We've killed the human soul, and the sword of science has been our murder weapon. Because, you see, in a world ruled by the empirical sciences, there's no room for the unseen. And since that pesky thing called a soul can't be seen under a microscope or weighed on a scale (the movie *21 Grams* not withstanding), well, we just had to conclude that it didn't exist—or shouldn't exist.

So we killed it.

Murdered by science and its sharp blade of materialism (the belief that matter is the only fundamental reality in the universe), the soul was misguidedly slaughtered in the name of reason.

Yet that *isn't* our Western heritage; the founders of Western philosophy never intended science veiled as reason to do away with the human soul. Quite the contrary; in the mystical philosophical traditions of antiquity, science and reason were embraced as tools that could elevate the soul towards the transcendent— not destroy it or deny its very existence. Indeed, rationalism in the form of reason and spirituality in the form of metaphysics weren't adversarial perspectives; they were *both* lenses that could illuminate a deeper truth. As was mentioned in the last chapter, this integral approach welcomed both science and spirituality at the table of knowledge.

In fact, in what some have described as a transrational perspective, the essence of philosophy for some of the most prominent Greek thinkers, such as Pythagoras, Parmenides, Plato, and Plotinus, was a mystical perspective that not only *included* reason, but also attempted to go *beyond* the logical constraints of reason and into a realm of expansive and ineffable paradox. These metaphysical philosophers have been described as *rational mystics*, which, to many, might be a term right up there with "military intelligence" as an oxymoron, but it's a very accurate—and seemingly contradictory—description.

Rational mysticism was an orientation that involved the use of the reasoning and the rational mind to achieve a higher level of metaphysical and mystical awareness that would then allow the practitioner to transcend the rational mind. By using reason, one could go *beyond* reason. These beyond-reason mystics viewed both mathematics and logic paradoxes as consciousness-expanding

How Plato and Pythagoras Can Save Your Life

keys that could unlock the door of the infinite and strangely paradoxical realm of Ultimate Reality.

Just as a Zen koan challenges the initiate to go beyond rational analysis, so too did these logic paradoxes challenge the philosophical initiate in Greece to transcend the limitations of reason and logic for a deeper, more transrational understanding. For the Greeks, riddles, paradoxes, and enigmas helped to free an individual's mind from misconceptions created by an overdependence on either sensory perception or constraining logic. While logic and reason had their obvious utility, they also had their constraining shortcomings—shortcomings that logic riddles would serve to expose.

For example, Zeno's "Achilles and the Tortoise" riddle forces us to reexamine our notions of motion and movement and, in a deeper sense, our ideas of space and time. In essence, Zeno and his teacher, Parmenides, wanted us to reexamine whether or not all of these things were merely illusions, or human constructs developed by a reasoning and ordered mind in order to measure things that really didn't exist independent of human thought and perception.

For the mystics (as well as for certain physicists), what we would call past, present, and future all coexist in what has been called the *eternal now*. Physicist Brian Greene discusses this difficult-to-grasp concept through the lens of physics and the totality of the universe as *spacetime*. Unlike the relativity of space and time, spacetime is absolute, meaning it contains all there is. Greene describes the totality of the spacetime universe as a huge, fresh loaf of bread. In this conception, past, present, and future are all baked into the loaf. You can slice the loaf a million different ways. It's the subjective angle of each slice that we cut out with our individual perception that determines what we perceive as that moment in time.

Logic Paradoxes:
Achilles and the Tortoise

Zeno was the student of the rational mystic philosopher Parmenides and is credited with creating several clever logic riddles. Let's take a look at his most famous one, ~~Achilles and the Tortoise~~, where the very idea of motion is challenged. In this riddle, the legendary Greek warrior Achilles is racing a slow-moving tortoise.

Zeno's riddle says that because the slow tortoise received a head start, the speedy Achilles will never catch it. This conclusion is in accordance with the rule of logic that says that for something to move between two points, it must first move halfway between those two points. But before it can traverse the first half distance, it must move half of that half, and half of that half, in turn, and so on, *ad infinitum.*

By this logic, a person, or in the case of Zeno's riddle, Achilles, can never reach the other point, which in this case is the tortoise that he is racing, because he will always be halving the distance into decreasingly smaller and more infinitesimal fractions. But these fractions will nonetheless always have some positive value greater than zero—meaning that he will never quite reach that other point (the tortoise).

Obviously Achilles will reach and surpass the tortoise; our senses and our experience confirm this. Yet logically, he shouldn't.

What sense are we to make of Zeno's riddle? As historian Bryan Magee writes in *The History of Thought* (1998):

continued

How Plato and Pythagoras Can Save Your Life

The point is that here is an impeccably logical argument that leads to a false conclusion. And what are we to say about that? If it is possible for us to start from unobjectionable premises, and then proceed by logical steps, each of which is without fault, to a conclusion that is manifestly untrue, this threatens with chaos all our attempts to reason about the world around us. People have found it terribly disconcerting. There must be a fault in the logic, they have said. But no one has yet been wholly successful in demonstrating what it is.

And that's the point; the purpose is to create a "crack in the constraining shell of the familiar, through which new worlds could be glimpsed" (Hoffman, 2004). These cracks are cracks in our familiar rational and logical constructs that allow an expansion of our consciousness into the "new world" of the transrational.

If we were a worm eating our way forward through the absolute spacetime loaf of the universe, gnawing forward from slice to slice, it's not time that's moving—it's us as the worm that's moving and experiencing things sequentially, thus giving us the illusion of the forward arrow of time.

But Greene doesn't address the questions that might be best left for philosophers and theologians: who baked the damn thing anyway?

I'll bet that you thought I was going to say God. Well, our friends the mystics didn't so much believe in *a* god as much as they believed that everything *is* God. In their conception, God is not the anthropormorphic old man with the white beard and cane; instead, God is just another word for the totality of the universe (the whole loaf of bread, even the part beyond the crust) —otherwise known as what we've been calling Ultimate Reality.

But what made the rational mystics of ancient Greece radically different from religious mystics was their use of reason to achieve the higher transrational awareness that I've described. While other mystics used certain prayers, religious meditations, or, in the case of Zen, an "empty cup," non-thinking meditation, the rational mystics embraced the abilities of the mind as the royal road towards Ultimate Reality.

Before we proceed any further, perhaps a few definitions are in order, since terms like *metaphysics* and *mysticism* often suffer from popular misconceptions.

Let's start with *metaphysics*. What does that mean? For some, the word *metaphysics* conjures up images of tarot cards, crystals, and tea leaves, dubious New Age practices used in incense-laden parlors, where a bejeweled and turbaned clairvoyant predicts the future. But that's *not* what I'm referring to when I use the term *metaphysics*. Nor am I referring to the Ms. Cleos and all the 1-800 psychic hotlines and their various permutations. While I'm not intending to disparage any of those things, they don't represent metaphysics in the classical Greek sense.

The ancient Greeks meant something altogether different when Aristotle first coined the phrase in his classic work *Metaphysics*.

Since it followed his treatise on nature and the physical world, entitled *Physics*, the title *Metaphysics* literally translates into "after physics" (*meta* is the Greek word for "after"). But Aristotle meant more by the term than just that *Metaphysics* came temporally after his earlier work; rather, it also implied that the metaphysical realm comes after physics in the sense that it is *more than* physics (the physical realm). *Metaphysics*, then, connotes an unseen, nonphysical, and nonmaterial reality that is *beyond* or *after* (*meta*) the physical.

Webster's dictionary (2007) defines the word *metaphysical* as "immaterial" and "incorporeal" and further defines *metaphysics* as "the branch of philosophy that systematically investigates the nature of first principles and problems of ultimate reality, including ontology and often cosmology."

Obviously, this is more than just reading tea leaves.

The Webster's definition also mentions *cosmology* and *ontology*, but what do those two words mean? Well, *cosmology* shouldn't be confused with the similarly sounding *cosmetology*. The latter has to do with hairstyling and weaves, while the former has to do with the study of the universe. It's also important to point out that when we refer to cosmology as the study of the universe, it's meant in both the philosophical and astrophysical sense. Thus, cosmology is the realm of *both* the astrophysicist and the philosopher.

Ontology is, quite simply, the study of being. The study of being? The study of being what? Well, the term *being*, in the ontological sense, is derived from the Greek word *ousia*, which, roughly translated, meant "essence" or "substance." So ontology, then, is the study of the essence of being, or in other words, an exploration into the nature of reality and existence. In fact, you might find it helpful to mentally substitute the word *existence* or *reality* whenever you see the word *being* discussed in philosophy books.

In any event, ontology examines what can exist and what cannot exist, and it further breaks those distinctions down into categories as it explores whether things can change or are, in fact, eternal.

These conceptions of "being" as an eternal and unchanging reality (also known as monistic orientations) versus "becoming," which is a dynamic, fluid process (also known as ontological pluralism), have been explored by both ancient philosophers, such as Heraclitus, Parmenides, and Aristotle, and their more modern counterparts, like German philosophers Edmund Husserl and Martin Heidegger.

So what about mysticism? What's that all about?

Mystics have been described as those spiritual seekers who seek to directly experience what some have called God or what others have called Ultimate Reality. That's the main point about our friends the mystics: they don't just want to read about God (or Ultimate Reality); they want to *experience* God. They want to *feel* Ultimate Reality.

The other key point about the mystic is the idea that true mystics don't believe that there's any separation between everything that exists and what God is; in other words, there's no dualistic divide between the infinite and the finite. God, or Ultimate Reality, *is the allness* of the universe. Many who share this orientation believe that we need to get out of our own way before we can *experience* what's all around us, that our senses, emotions, and, yes, our discursive thinking can actually cloud us from experiencing this allness.

I'm reminded of the parable of the fish that doesn't believe in water.

How Plato and Pythagoras Can Save Your Life

"I don't believe in this thing you call water!" exclaimed the skeptical fish. "I can't see it. I can't touch it. Prove to me that there is such a thing!"

With that, an older and much wiser fish, which had been swimming by and had overheard the skeptical fish, stopped and shook his head (as fish that inhabit the world of parables can sometimes do). He calmly replied, "You don't see water, yet it's all around you. You don't experience it because your mind won't allow you to!"

While the mystics would agree with the sage fish's perspective that the unseeable is "all around us," they also, as I've mentioned, believe that everything *is* God—or Ultimate Reality. Huston Smith, the eminent MIT and Berkeley professor who's widely considered one of the world's preeminent authorities on comparative religions, describes the mystic's belief this way: "For the atheist, there is no God; for the polytheist, there are many Gods; for the monotheist, there is only one God; for the mystic, there is *only* God" (Smith, 2001).

Mystics tend to shy away from religious sacraments and dogma in their search for a more personal and direct union with the infinite. How does the mystic find that union? How does he or she tap into the numinous? Well, for many, this magic carpet ride is often achieved via deep contemplative meditation of a usually solitary nature. Yet while the journey for the typical mystic tends to be an individual and lone path, most major religions have mystical branches (usually as ascetic or contemplative monastic orders): Buddhism has Zen, Islam has Sufism, Judaism has the Kabbalah, Christianity has the St. John of the Cross or St. Ignatius traditions, and so on.

Regardless of whether a person is part of a monastic sect or just a lone-wolf nature mystic, his or her mystical quest tends to be a search for a more expansive level of reality—the metaphysical *more*, no matter what it's called (God or Ultimate Reality). *That* seems to be the mystic's Holy Grail. (My apologies for mixing religious metaphors.)

All right then, enough talk about these mystics in the abstract. Who exactly were these Greek mystics and what were they all about?

How Plato and Pythagoras Can Save Your Life

Exercise 7

Beyond Logic: Riddles and Paradoxes

This contemplative exercise deals with **paradigm-shattering riddles and paradoxes.** As discussed in this chapter, the Greeks valued riddles and paradoxes because they could **"create a crack in the constraining shell of the familiar, through which new worlds could be glimpsed."** In other words, riddles and paradoxes can open up our minds and expand our consciousness in order to get us past habituated ways of thinking.

For this exercise, we are going to contemplate two interesting riddles—one from the world of quantum physics and one from Japanese philosophy.

But before we begin, **take a few minutes to do some sort of physical exercise,** being sure to only do as much as your physical health allows. This could include **walking, jogging, or bicycling.** After **fifteen to thirty minutes** (depending on your health) of exercise, **find a body of water to sit facing in quiet contemplation.** This can be a pond, a river, a lake, or a pool. If there are no appropriate bodies of water, light a candle and meditate while focusing on the flickering flame.

For our first meditation, let us examine the **Heisenberg Principle** from quantum physics. This principle states that, depending on the kind of observation, **light** could manifest as either a **particle** (little packets of energy) or a **wave** with all the appropriate wave functions. **But how can something be two things at once?** How can something seem to be *both* a particle and a wave, yet not manifest as either until it is observed?

Along the same theme regarding **participant-observer effects** (as they have been dubbed or, as others call them, Creator-created dynamics), let's meditate on the old **Zen koan** about the tree falling in the forest: **If a tree falls in the forest and there's no one there to hear it, does it make**

a sound? And even if it did create a sound wave, **how would that sound manifest if there is no eardrum to process it?** Take several minutes to contemplate this notion.

When you're done, sit for several more moments and become aware of how you feel. Now look around you; do you experience things any differently? **Feel free to write down any of these initial thoughts and feelings,** as writing these down will help you to process this experience.

PART FOUR

Pythagoras, the Big Beat, and Cosmic Consciousness

The so-called miraculous powers of a great master are a natural accompaniment to his exact understanding of subtle laws that operate in the inner cosmos of consciousness.

—Sri Paramahansa Yogananda

It's such an extraordinary thing, music. It is how we speak to God finally—or how we don't. Even if we're ignoring God.
It's the language of the spirit. If you believe that we contain within our skin and bones a spirit that might last longer than your time breathing in and out—if there is a spirit, music is the thing that wakes it up. And it certainly woke up mine. And it seems to be how we communicate on another level.

—Bono

Music is well said to be the speech of angels;
in fact, nothing among the utterances allowed to man is felt to be so divine. It brings us near to the Infinite.

—Thomas Carlyle

Pythagoras Squared:
Who Was This Mystic Mathemagician?

If I mention the name *Pythagoras*, what's the first thing that pops into your mind? Most people think of him as an ancient mathematician that developed that little triangle theorem most of us were forced to learn in school. When most of us think of a mathematician, images of slide rules, greasy hair, horned-rimmed glasses, and pocket organizers come to mind. Add *ancient* to *mathematician*, and we tend to wrap our stereotypical image in an off-the-shoulder toga; he's still a math geek, only in a looser outfit.

But Pythagoras was not your typical math geek; in fact, he was much, much more than just a mathematician. He was also a musician, as well as a philosopher (whom, as I mentioned earlier, some have credited with being the first to use the word *philosopher*, Greek for "lover of wisdom"). And unlike the dry and cerebral academics who pass themselves off as philosophers today, Pythagoras was a metaphysician, the trippiest kind of philosopher.

Today's somnolent philosophy professors tend to be painfully rational creatures who are detached from life and lost in books as they explore philosophy as a form of intellectual exercise. For them, philosophy is some arcane form of cerebral calisthenics, meant to be performed in an academic tower or in a university library. But that's *not* what philosophy was for the mystically oriented metaphysicians. These lovers of wisdom believed in—and sought—a deeper level of reality through the purification and *lived* practice of philosophy. And in stark contrast to today's fragmented and compartmentalized age, Pythagoras and his followers sought this consciousness-elevating wisdom in all of its many-flowered varieties—mathematical, musical, creative, intuitive, scientific, contemplative, rational, and ethical. Today, many would find it almost sacrilegious, if not simply bizarre, to combine all of those lenses in an integrated approach.

But Pythagoras and his followers embraced many beliefs and practices that would probably seem pretty strange to most of us. In fact, it might even be fair to say that by many of today's standards, Pythagoras would be considered an eccentric who was quite out there. I mean, how else would you describe an ancient Greek who wore pants (in a world of togas), claimed to be able to communicate with animals (a la Dr. Doolittle), and not only believed that the universe was essentially vibrational, but also claimed to be able to hear those cosmic, Brian Wilson–like good vibrations? Now add to those eccentricities his passionate belief in reincarnation (he could vividly and descriptively recall his past lives) and his insistence that all of his followers be fig-eating semi-vegetarians who needed to engage in daily memory exercises, lyre playing, rigorous physical exercise, and, of course, mathematical and philosophical contemplation in order to purify their soul and experience the unseen yet underlying framework of reality.

Pretty trippy stuff, no?

But Pythagoras and his followers did indeed believe that as a result of their lifestyle, they just might be able to pull back the veil and see the face of God (or experience Ultimate Reality). I think it would be pretty fair to say that Pythagoras was old-school New Age.

But things with Pythagoras get even funkier. There are the tales of his miracles. I'm not kidding; there are descriptions in the historical record of Pythagoras as a Christ-like miracle worker. These include fantastic stories about Pythagoras traveling to the underworld of the dead, about the music of his lyre healing the sick, about him patting a predatory bear and convincing it to become a vegetarian, about him whispering into an ox's ear and convincing it to no longer eat beans, and about him winning a wager by being able to correctly predict the number of fish in a fisherman's net and then asking for the fish to be released back into the ocean.

Then there were the tales of his bilocation. His bi-what? His bilocation: the supposed mystic ability to be at two places at once. Pythagoras was allegedly documented by witnesses to have been both at Metapontum in Italy and Tauromenium in Sicily on the same day and at the exact same time. And no, he didn't have Scotty's transporter beam, nor did he have a prank-playing twin.

Oh yeah, he also knew two thousand years before Galileo that the earth revolved around the sun. But, unlike Galileo, he figured it out without a telescope.

Now even if, for argument sake, we throw out the miracle stories of bilocation and such, we're still left with an amazing man who somehow intuited aspects of the universe (which we'll talk more about in a bit) without the aid of any of the toys of modern science.

How was this possible?

Well, before we get into the how of Pythagoras and his wisdom, let's take a look at the who of Pythagoras. Just who was this mystical mathemagician?

Getting an accurate picture of the historical Pythagoras is complicated by the fact that he didn't write anything, nor were his students allowed to write anything. Later philosophers like Socrates didn't believe in writing down their philosophical beliefs because they felt that philosophy should be *lived* rather than written about.

In Pythagoras's case, political persecution is also believed to have played an important role in the secrecy of his sect, which, by some estimates, numbered over 2,500 members while he was alive and was said to have grown significantly in popularity after his death. Pythagoreanism would influence later generations of philosophers, including Plato and Plotinus.

Since we don't have anything written from the period when he lived, everything that we know about both his life and his teachings comes down to us many years after the fact, and some accounts were written as many as several hundred years after Pythagoras's lifetime. (This is, unfortunately, very often the case with important historical figures; what we know of them very rarely comes from sources written in their own hand or by contemporaries. Another prominent example of someone we know only by second-hand historical sourcing is Jesus Christ. Many Christians are unaware that the gospels of the New Testament weren't written by Christ's contemporaries, but, instead, by Christian devotees years after his life.) Most of the written accounts about Pythagoras's teachings and his life are from the biographer of philosophers Diogenes Laertius and the neoplatonists Porphyr of Tyre and Iamblichus of Chalcis, who were authors from the third and fourth centuries CE (see "Chronological Chart of Sources for Pythagoras"). The works of these writers, along with earlier writings from Plato and Aristotle that reference Pythagoras and the Pythagoreans, provide us with all of our existing knowledge of Pythagoras.

Unfortunately, the information from these sources is often uneven and sometimes even contradictory. And here's the real problem: How much of these historical accounts are exaggerated myths and how many are factual? Where does the historical Pythagoras end and the mythologized legend begin?

Chronological Chart of Sources for Pythagoras

Time Period	Philosopher, Author, or Texts	Description or Title
500 BCE	Pythagoras (570–490 BCE)	The source
400 BCE	Plato (427–347 BCE) and Aristotle (384-322 BCE)	
300 BCE	Timaeus of Tauromenium (350–260 BCE)	Historian of Sicily
200 BCE	Pythagorean Memoirs (200 BCE)	Sections quoted by Diogenes Laertius.
100 BCE	Alexander Polyhistor (b. 105 BCE)	His excerpts of the Pythagorean Memoirs are quoted by Diogenes Laertius.
	Pseudo-Pythagorean texts forged	Starting as early as 300 BCE, but most common in the first century BCE

continued

Time Period	Philosopher, Author, or Texts	Description or Title
100 BCE	Aetius (first century CE)	*Opinions of the Philosophers* (reconstructed by H. Diels from pseudo-Plutarch, *Opinions of the Philosophers* [second century CE] and Stobaeus, *Selections* [fifth century CE])
	Moderatus of Gades (50–100 CE)	*Lectures on Pythagoreanism* (fragments quoted in Porphyry)
	Apollonius of Tyana (d. ca. 97 CE)	*Life of Pythagoras* (fragments quoted in Iamblichus and others)
100 CE	Nicomachus (ca. 50–150 CE)	*Introduction to Arithmetic* (extant), *Life of Pythagoras* (fragments quoted in Iamblichus and others)
200 CE	Sextus Empiricus	(summaries of Pythagoras's philosophy in *Adversus Mathematicos* [Against the Theoreticians], circa 200 CE)
	Diogenes Laertius (ca. 200–250 CE)	*Life of Pythagoras* (extant)
	Porphyry (234–ca. 305 CE)	*Life of Pythagoras* (extant)
300 CE	Iamblichus (ca. 245–325 CE)	*On the Pythagorean Life* (extant)

How Plato and Pythagoras Can Save Your Life

We know that Pythagoras was born approximately 580 BCE in Samos, Ionia (on what would now be the western coast of Turkey). The rest gets a little murky; I think it's fair to say his deification begins immediately with the miraculous stories of his birth.

When Iamblichus, in his *On the Pythagorean Life*, writes about Pythagoras's childhood, he gives us a description of a rather Jesus-like divine birth. The story is replete with an immaculate conception (in this version, Apollo plays the role of inseminating divinity) and a much-prophesized birth to a mother whose name, Parthenis, is Greek for "virginal." Many historians have pointed out the archetypal aspects of this type of birth, along with the chosen one's subsequent trips to the underworld and accompanying resurrection mythology. This archetype—which most in the West associate with Jesus—actually has even more ancient origins: in the stories of Osiris in Egypt, Mithra in Persia, Adonis and Attis in Syria, Krishna in India, and Hercules in ancient Greece, we see these same common themes.

Myths and Miracles

In discussions of quasi-deified historical figures like Pythagoras, it may be reasonable to quibble over what is fact and what is myth. Lord knows that in attempting to discern between the two, I've often asked myself, can these far-fetched stories possibly be true? Is there any room for exceptional abilities bordering on the miraculous in the lives of these types of transformational figures?

My conclusion? To loosely paraphrase Socrates, the only thing that I really do know is that I really don't know. How can I know when I wasn't there? But as we saw in our earlier

continued

---

discussion from chapter 3, wherein we discussed some truly logic-defying abilities of what we had called human white crows (e.g., savants, healers, remote viewers), I don't think we can automatically dismiss tales of unusual abilities out of hand, especially given some of the more recent discoveries of the "new science."

Increasingly, science, in the form of quantum mechanics and consciousness research, opens doors that seem to defy not only our sensory experience, but also logic itself. Indeed, the more we discover in the realm of quantum mechanics, the more we enter a disquieting world of paradigm-rocking paradox (some of which we'll discuss in chapter 15: "New Science and Ancient Wisdom"). Given how quickly we're discovering that the universe is full of surprises, I don't believe that it's wise to dismiss anything with absolute certainty.

The other, less-credulity-straining explanation for some of the seemingly supernatural descriptions for revered historical figures like Pythagoras is the more mundane human tendency to project godlike mythical qualities on our heroes in order to quench our insatiable thirst for myth. Why do so many cultures not only embrace creation myths, but also have, as part of their cultural fabric, stories of divinities inseminating a virgin to create a hybrid man-god? Well, one explanation has been that these stories give a narrative to the universally held belief that humans contain a divine aspect, or spark; what better way to express that idea than by saying that we are the offspring of a divine union?

continued

I think we also need to acknowledge that we moderns of the twenty-first century tend to take a rather snide and condescending view of the whole notion of this thing called mythology; we really don't seem to get it, because we often look at many of the world's mythologies *literally.* "Ha, ha," we smugly snicker. "How quaint of the primitives to believe in fairy tales and sun gods and to have harvest festivals, or to believe that the world was created in six days. How very absurd!"

But pioneering psychologist Carl Jung and his devotee, the wonderful Joseph Campbell, wrote dense texts describing not only the archetypal aspects of myth, but also the *importance* of myth to the human psyche. Myths and their archetypes might not be just important to our psyche as explanatory "creation stories"; they might, in fact, be the very *embodiment* of our collective psyche, or what Jung termed our *collective unconscious.*

In his time, Jung lamented that humanity was experiencing a dearth (what he called "a poverty") of symbols and meaning, two critically important, humanity-sustaining elements that myths had effectively nourished. Unfortunately, our psyche today is still malnourished, as myths have gone the way of the dinosaurs in our demystified modern world. Alas, it was we, the sophisticated moderns, with our constraining weapon of science serving as our WMSD (weapons of mass spiritual destruction) who killed God and the soul—and myth.

The killing of myth has been to our societal detriment because we *need* our myths; we need our explanatory tales to

continued

help us not only make sense of the world, but also, perhaps, tap into a collective wisdom or source—Jung's collective unconscious, which, as we shall soon see, is not all that different from Plato's Ideal Realm.

In 2010, James Cameron's film *Avatar* had just passed the one-billion-dollar mark in worldwide sales to become the highest-grossing film of all time, and it has been lauded as a cultural phenomenon. But what is *Avatar* if not an archetypal myth writ large in IMAX, 3-D splendor? In *Avatar* we have the quintessential *hero's journey*, the ancient and cross-cultural archetype described by Joseph Campbell in *The Hero with a Thousand Faces* (1949). We have a hero who has to overcome obstacles and cross various thresholds to achieve some transformational goal that's the object of his quest.

Campbell identifies universal stages in this quest, including the hero's "call to adventure," where the hero ventures out from his world into a region of "supernatural wonder." The hero crosses thresholds into the unknown and undergoes various initiation rites on his ultimate journey of "apotheosis," the alchemical transformation that he achieves after traveling into the underworld (or experiencing a physical death). That transformation then leads to his supernatural deification, or "bliss," through "divine knowledge."

Isn't that hero's quest the plot of *Avatar*?

Yes, like religion, myths do offer some psychological soothing. But whether myths act as soothing opiates, as explanatory frameworks to give our world meaning, or as

continued

How Plato and Pythagoras Can Save Your Life

expressions of our bubbling collective unconscious, it really would seem that they play a sustaining and vitally important role in the human psyche.

So, again, are the "miraculous" biographical details of Pythagoras's life historical facts that can perhaps be explained by the new science, or are they merely mythologized artifacts projected onto a revered historical figure in order to satisfy the powerful human psyche's need for myth? I know that I don't know for sure whether the messenger is mythologized or an actual miracle worker; nonetheless, the message itself is still pretty amazing. And, after all, isn't there room in our wondrous universe for both myth and miracle?

For Pythagoras's deity-inspired birth, Iamblichus describes how the Pythia (the priestess presiding over the oracle of Apollo at Delphi) told Mnesarchos, Pythagoras's traveling-salesman father, who was in Delphi on a business trip, that he would have a very financially successful trip and that his beautiful wife would soon give birth to a child that would surpass all humans for beauty and wisdom and would be of the greatest benefit to the human race. Excited by this prophecy, Mnesarchos is said to have immediately changed his wife's name from Parthenis to Pythia in honor of the oracle at Delphi. Continuing with the Pythian inspiration, he also named his son Pythagoras.

To be fair, Iamblichus rejects the notion (originally presented by earlier writers, such as Epimenides, Eudoxus, and Xenocrates) that Pythagoras's birth had actually been a result of Apollo's, ahem, influence. But regardless of whether or not Pythagoras was actually the son of the sun god, he would forever be associated with the myth and legend of Apollo. Indeed, many of Pythagoras's beliefs and teachings would indeed reflect an Apollonian orientation.

After Pythagoras's father, Mnesarchus, returned home to Samos, he built a temple in honor of Apollo and, assured by the oracle that his newborn child would be quite special, made sure that the boy received the best possible education, replete with oratory lessons, Homeric poetry, and the subtleties of lyre playing. But he was also versed in all matters divine; he studied and trained under the local Samian priests, since Mnesarchus understood that such a golden child needed to have both his mind and soul equally well cultivated.

Unfortunately, Mnesarchus would die while Pythagoras was still quite young, but he had succeeded in raising his son to indeed be very special. The young and gifted Pythagoras attained a revered status in Samos. And, according to the various records, Pythagoras was quite the Brad Pitt of his day, described as "the most beautiful and god-like of all those who have been celebrated in the annals of history." But his beauty was more than just skin deep; as Iamblichus describes it:

> After his father's death, though he was still a youth, his aspect was so venerable, and his habits so temperate that he was honored and even revered by elderly men, attracting the attention of all who heard him speak, creating the most profound impression. That is the reason that many plausibly asserted that he was a child of the divinity.
>
> Enjoying the privilege of such renown, of an education so thorough from infancy, and of so impressive

a natural appearance he showed that he deserved all these advantages by deserving them, by the adornment of piety and discipline, by exquisite habits, by firmness of soul, and by a body duly subjected to the mandates of reason. An inimitable quiet and serenity marked all his words and actions, soaring above all laughter, emulation, contention, or any other irregularity or eccentricity; his influence at Samos was that of some beneficent divinity.

His great renown, while yet a youth, reached not only men as illustrious for their wisdom as Thales of Miletus, and Bias at Prione, but also extended to the neighboring cities. He was celebrated everywhere as the "long haired Samian," and by the multitude was given credit for being under divine inspiration.

So not only did he have Brad Pitt looks and rock-star notoriety, but he was also a "firm soul" who was pious, disciplined, and even tempered.

Yet with fame and notoriety comes a price. When Pythagoras turned eighteen, the tyrant Polycrates gained control of the region, and, fearing that he wouldn't be able to study freely anymore, Pythagoras decided that it was time to leave his home island of Samos. He traveled to nearby Miletus, already established by that time as a hotbed of deep thinking, as it was the home of Thales (the "first" Greek philosopher and the founder of Ionian tradition that was flourishing in Miletus).

Thales was duly impressed by the young "long haired Samian" and accepted him readily into his inner circle. In addition to learning mathematical and intellectual insights from Thales, Pythagoras also learned some healthy lifestyle habits from the sage old man. Again, we refer to Iamblichus: "Pythagoras had benefited from the instruction of Thales in many respects, but his greatest lesson had been to learn the value of saving time, which led him to abstain entirely from wine and animal food, avoiding greediness, confining himself to nutrients of easy preparation and digestion. As a result, his sleep was short, his soul pure and vigilant, and the general health of his body was invariable." But Thales was approaching sixty years of age and, unlike Pythagoras, was not in the best of health; thus, his ability to educate the young and eager Samian was limited. Realizing that the young Pythagoras was a special student that would benefit from more instruction, Thales suggested that he travel to Memphis, the thriving Egyptian city on the west bank of the Nile that was famous for its wise priests—the very same priests who had trained Thales as a younger man.

So off to Egypt went Pythagoras. He studied extensively at Memphis and later in Diospolis (also known as Thebes), where he would eventually become an initiate and disciple in that city's holy temple.

It was in Egypt, the ancient land of the Great Pyramids, that Pythagoras is believed by many historians to have learned his esoteric and mystical wisdom. Indeed, some have suggested that to know Pythagoreanism is to know the Egyptian mysteries. Thus, one might say that the tree of Greek metaphysics has its roots in the land of the Nile (see "Pythagorian Mysticism: All Roads Lead to Egypt").

Pythagorean Mysticism: All Roads Lead to Egypt

Who woulda thunk that the road to Athens makes a pit stop at the Pyramids? Really, when the average person thinks "Greek philosophy," they don't tend to think of Cleopatra and the land of the Nile.

But I think it's fair to say that if Western civilization is standing on Plato's broad shoulders—and that Plato is standing on Pythagoras's somewhat more wiry shoulders— well, then, Pythagoras is standing on top of a pyramid. And, as I'll explain, he might have *literally* been straddling a little pyramid power.

Ancient Egypt remains a huge mystery for Westerners; most know the Great Pyramids in Giza. In fact, there are a total of six pyramid sites. But we scarcely know how and, more importantly, why they were built. The explanation that the pyramids are pharaoh tombs has remained unsatisfying to many Egyptologists, many of whom have recently embraced a new perspective about ancient Egyptians that might shed some light on the actual purpose of the Pyramids. What's more, these new insights into the Egyptians can also illuminate ancient Greek mysticism as practiced by Pythagoras.

Since most historians agree that Pythagoras was initiated into the priesthood in Diospolis (Thebes) and also spent significant time in Memphis, it should be fair to assume that Egyptian teachings shaped his early views of cosmology. And, sure enough, when we see the parallels between Pythagoreanism and Egyptian beliefs, the relationship becomes fairly clear. Both the Egyptian priests and

continued

Pythagoras were ritual vegetarians, both believed in metempsychosis (reincarnation), both embraced mathematics and astronomy, and both believed in incubation death rituals. But, as we'll soon discover, there was quite a bit more to Egyptian beliefs than pyramids-as-tombs and a reincarnation obsession.

To know the ancient Egyptian way is, I believe, to know Pythagoras. But what did the ancient Egyptians believe? What were they all about? For centuries, the sands of Egypt had covered it in mystery. The country is ancient—some believe far more ancient than orthodox Egyptology acknowledges—and still strangely unknown to us. Yet in the nineteenth and twentieth centuries, incredible archaeological discoveries were uncovered from the depths of white sand. Pyramids, tombs, sarcophaguses, obelisks—like phantoms from the past, they emerged into the desert sun.

We have long thought that the Egyptians were obsessed with death, and they were. Although, strangely, there was no word in ancient Egyptian for death. Instead, when a person died, he or she was said to be "westing." (No, that's not Elmer Fudd saying "resting"); the Egyptians believed that, just as the sun set in the west only to be reborn in the east the following morning, so too was the person "westing," only to be soon reborn again.

But the notion that all of the fantastic pyramids that had been built throughout Egypt were just fancy tombs has recently received a lot of criticism. Egyptologist Carmen Boulter of the University of Calgary just recently filmed a five-part documentary entitled *The Pyramid*

continued

How Plato and Pythagoras Can Save Your Life

Code wherein she dispels the notions of the Pyramids as grandiose coffins. Not only do the various pyramids have astronomical importance in terms of their positioning (with special significance given to Orion and Sirius), but Boulter claims that the Pyramids were also, in fact, sophisticated harmonic structures!

More Pythagorean parallels, anyone?

In her documentary, Boulter interviews Abdel Hakim Awyan, an Egyptian archaelogist and indigenous wisdom keeper. The grizzled old man explains that all the chambers of the Pyramids had harmonic properties. Other experts have since confirmed that the Pyramids were indeed constructed with harmonics in mind.

Those are pretty big tuning forks. The Great Pyramid in Giza covers thirteen acres and comprises over 2.3 million stones, each weighing up to 200 tons; that's a pretty big subwoofer. What could these harmonic pyramids have possibly been used for?

Boulter, Awyan, and author Graham Hancock believe they were used harmonically in two ways. First of all, they were used as healing centers. The sick and ailing would come to these vibrational centers for, literally, a tune-up; if you weren't vibrating properly and were out of sync with health—and, thus, ill—well then, there was nothing like a little pyramid power to do the trick.

Keep in mind that these six geographically separated pyramid sites were connected via no-longer-visible waterways, which added hydropower to the pyramid effect. And metallurgists indicate that the various pyramids were coated

continued

with very specific and very different metals, the properties of which added to the energetic effect.

What was the second use of this network of pyramids? Are you ready Pythagoreans? Consciousness expansion— on a global level.

John Dering, an electromagnetic-field theorist, suggests that the Pyramids synergistically combined (perhaps also with the other pyramid sites in places such as Peru and China) to create a global shift in electromagnetism—an astounding, planetary-wide frequency vibration that could alter states of consciousness and shift a person's frequency, so that one could explore "the realm beyond death."

Boulter believes that ancient wisdom keepers created mystery schools and priesthoods. (Pythagoras quite possibly had been trained in these schools. That would explain his focus on all things vibrational.) Awyan, the modern wisdom keeper, indicates that, according to the wisdom that's been passed down to him, the ancients had mastered sound and vibration; indeed, legend has it that the megalithic stones used to build the Pyramids were moved not by rope and pulley, but by sound.

Awyan also claims that we, as humans, have lost many abilities that we once had; he claims that his ancestors are alleged to have had "360 senses," which have atrophied in modern humans due to lack of use.

The truth regarding ancient Egypt may always be somewhat unclear. However, what does seem clear is that Pythagoras entered the land of the Pyramids and left with a new mystical practice based on vibration and sound.

Not surprisingly, some have suggested that it is this extensive training under the Egyptians that can explain Pythagoras's appreciation and knowledge of mathematical and geometric concepts. That certainly seems reasonable as the Egyptians during this time were quite advanced in mathematics and astronomy; thus, it seems logical that anybody studying in Egypt at that time would be exposed to such teachings. Certainly Thales had absorbed much of his mathematical training in Egypt and was said to have confided as much to Pythagoras before the latter left for Memphis.

Unfortunately, Pythagoras's time in Egypt was interrupted by the geopolitics of the day. Persia invaded Egypt in 525 BCE, and the Persian king Cambyses II's naval victory in the battle of Pelusium in the Nile delta would lead to the capture Heliopolis and Memphis. Caught up in the conflict, Pythagoras was taken captive and carried off to Babylon. But Pythagoras was a special light; he soon was embraced by his Babylonian captors and allowed to study with their *magi* ("wise men"), being taught their sacred wisdom. It was in Babylon that Pythagoras is said to have studied with—and been influenced by—the Persian philosopher and religious poet Zoroaster, the founder of Zoroastrianism.

Zoroaster saw the human condition as the mental struggle between *aša* ("truth") and *druj* ("lie"). According to Zoroaster, it was our purpose to sustain *aša* through active participation in life and the exercise of constructive thoughts, words, and deeds. These teachings are believed to have greatly influenced the still-quite-young Pythagoras; indeed, some historians believe that it was Zoroaster who had the greatest influence on Pythagoras's ideas of philosophy as purification. As Porphyr describes it: "In Babylon he associated with the other Chaldeans, especially attaching himself to

Zaratus [Zoroaster], by whom he was purified from the pollutions of his past life, and taught the things from which a virtuous man ought to be free. Likewise he heard lectures about Nature and the principles of wholes. It was from his stay among these foreigners that Pythagoras acquired the greatest part of his wisdom . . ."

In approximately 520 BCE, Pythagoras left Babylon and returned home to his native Samos, where he quickly formed a school known as "the semicircle." Again we refer to Iamblichus: "[H]e formed a school in the city [of Samos], the 'semicircle' of Pythagoras . . . in which the Samians hold political meetings. They do this because they think one should discuss questions about goodness, justice and expediency in this place which was founded by the man who made all these subjects his business. Outside the city he made a cave the private site of his own philosophical teaching, spending most of the night and daytime there and doing research into the use of mathematics . . ."

So we see that it was back in his native Samos that Pythagoras began to develop a following and where he first planted the seeds of what would become known as Pythagoreanism.

But Pythagoras soon left Samos allegedly because his frustration with local ignorance that led to a rejection of his teaching methods. As Iamblichus describes it: "[H]e tried to use his symbolic method of teaching which was similar in all respects to the lessons he had learned in Egypt. The Samians were not very keen on this method and treated him in a rude and improper manner."

Other sources indicate that, at age forty, Pythagoras left Samos not only because his teachings weren't embraced, but also to once again flee from political persecution. Seeking more tolerant and enlightened pastures, Pythagoras travelled and settled in Croton, a city on the southeastern heel of what's now Italy, but which was still, at that time, a Greek community.

How Plato and Pythagoras Can Save Your Life

It was here in Croton that Pythagoras and his movement flourished, as he formed an elite and disciplined society comprised of both male and female followers. This coed arrangement was quite shocking for ancient Greece, which was a rather sexist culture in which women were not considered on an equal footing with men.

The Pythagoreans were not your typical Greek community; theirs was a different sort of sensibility—an eclectic mix of mystic, hippie commune and a self-disciplined, military-style boot camp. This Shangri-La had been started by Pythagoras as an attempt to reform the cultural life of Croton. He urged people to follow virtue and live a strict and self-disciplined way of life—while tripping on contemplative mediation as a form of groovy mind expansion.

This ascetic-yet-trippy way of life became known as the *Bios Pythagorikos* (see the sidebar "Old-School Holistic: *The Bios Pythagorikos*") and required that all members of Pythagoras's "society" live ethically, love one another, practice pacifism, believe in reincarnation, become semivegetarians, devote themselves to *purification* via philosophy, and the embrace of the vibrational and mathematical nature of the universe.

As we will explore in more detail later in this chapter, their conception of what we call mathematics was not exactly what a math graduate student might study today. Indeed, their appreciation of math was quite a bit more abstract and related more to numbers as the underlying *principles* of existence with cosmological and theological overtones. Iamblichus quotes Pythagoras as saying, "Number is the ruler of forms and ideas and the cause of gods and demons." When's the last time you heard a math teacher say something like that about numbers?

However utopian the Pythagorean society aspired to be, it was not a homogeneous group, as there were two types of membership. The more elite inner circle, called the *Mathematikoi* (the "mathematicians"), was a very disciplined-yet-bohemian bunch that lived in communelike collectivism, eschewing personal possessions, as they resided on the Pythagorean campus. The second-tier Pythagoreans were commuters who lived in the neighboring villages and traveled to the society during the day; this commuter class was allowed to own property and was called the *Akousmatikoi* (the "listeners"), as they would hear the day's lessons retold to them by the inner circle.

Old-School Holistic:
The Bios Pythagorikos

Memory *(mneme)* and memory exercises were a big deal to the Pythagoreans. Not only were the exercises a form of mental and intellectual training, but memory was also essential aspect of reincarnation. The soul needed a good memory in order to recall the lessons of past lives and thus be able to choose the appropriate next life.

But there was something else about memory that made it very important to Pythagoras and the ancient Greeks. They believed that all knowledge could be remembered, that knowledge was contained within each individual and, with the right training, could be brought to the surface of conscious memory. Plato tells a famous story about Socrates pulling aside a young, uneducated slave boy, and, after Plato diagrammed a couple of rudimentary geometric ideas with a stick in the sand, the boy was able to "remember" *(anamnesis)* more advanced geometric concepts.

Since memory was such a big deal, no Pythagorean was supposed to get out of bed without recalling the events of the

continued

How Plato and Pythagoras Can Save Your Life

prior day, trying to repeat mentally the first thing he or she said or did, then the second, and so on, in an effort to sharpen their memories.

In addition to memory, music played an important role in the *Bios Pythagorikos*. The Pythagoreans woke up and went to sleep with the sweet melody of lyre playing. In the morning, they would "arouse their souls with the sound of the lyre" so that they could be more alert for their day. At night, lyre playing was used to calm their minds in case their thoughts were too turbulent.

Also very important were daily walks. Initially, a person would take a reflective morning walk alone to compose his or her thoughts. The Pythagoreans thought it was essential to not meet anyone until "their own soul [was] in order and [they] were composed in their intellect." After this morning alone time, they would gather in small groups for lessons, discussions, and contemplative meditations on philosophy, ethics, mathematics, and character development.

Once these intellectual and meditative pursuits were over, they turned their attention to their bodies; activities such as running, wrestling, and shadow boxing were chosen depending on each individual's particular strengths. This emphasis on a fit body also extended to Pythagoras's beliefs about diet. He felt diet was critically important and not just for the previously mentioned reincarnation purposes. Diet also had to do with a "sound body, sound mind" philosophical orientation. One's body, as the instrument that contained the soul, or the "higher aspect," had to be tuned properly, just like any other instrument. A rotted old violin that's not tuned

continued

properly, even if it's a Stradivarius, is not going to be able to produce the beautiful notes of a Vivaldi violin concerto.

And Pythagoras practiced what he preached. It was written that even as he became an old man (he is said to have died at age 100), he cut a lean and athletic figure: "[H]is body always maintained the same form, as if on a straight line; he was not sometimes well, sometimes ill, and also not sometimes fattened and sometimes losing weight and getting thinner."

No yo-yo dieting for Pythagoras. For breakfast, he prescribed honey and bread. (This was bread made from millet or barley; it was organic way before organic.) For the later meals, bread was once again served, with cooked or raw vegetables. Meat (and not from all parts of the animal) was to be eaten on rare occasions.

Pythagoras had also created a form of energy bar for those long hikes in the shrines. (The Pythagoreans maintained a respect for the deities of the day and often took long, multiday retreats to offer their worship.) One type of this power food helped make him "hunger free" (a-limos), while the other reduced his thirst (a-dipsos). The first was a paste that he made from honey, barley flour, and chickpeas, to which he then added poppy seed, sesame seed, mallow leaves, and squill. The thirst-free treat was raisins, cucumber seeds, grated cheese, wheat flour, and milk, all also mixed with honey. They sound like energy bars that could probably be on the shelf of your local health food store; they could be called something like Pythagoras Power, or maybe even P Squared.

continued

How Plato and Pythagoras Can Save Your Life

It was essentially this combination of a holistic lifestyle that comprised the *Bios Pythagorikos*, a way of life intended to purify or "retune" an individual so that they could experience the Big Beat of the Cosmic Harmony.

But there was definitely a sort of class warfare between the Mathematikoi and the Akousmatikoi. Porhyr wrote that while "the Mathematikoi learned the more detailed and exact elaborate version of this knowledge, the Akousmatikoi were those which had heard only the summary headings of his [Pythagoras's] writings, without the more exact exposition." In other words, the Mathematikoi got the real deal of Pythagoras's wisdom, while the commuter Akousmatikoi got thrown the superficial scraps. In fact, the Akousmatikoi were not even allowed to even see Pythagoras; that privilege was reserved for his inner circle of Mathematikoi.

And even amongst this inner circle there were severe restrictions; Mathematikoi initiates had to maintain a vow of silence for *five years* before they were allowed to fully become inner-circle members.

Silence for the Pythagoreans really was golden, as it was felt that *echemythia* ("silence") was a necessary virtue that an evolved and contemplative individual needed to develop before being taught the deeper mysteries.

But what were these deeper mysteries? What were these mystical magical teachings of Pythagoras really all about?

Exercise 8

Infinity: The Ultimate Mind Trip

This contemplative exercise deals with the nature of **infinity.** Huston Smith once said that **we can't even begin to conceive of the infinite because our minds are finite.** Perhaps so, but let us attempt to contemplate the concept of infinity nonetheless.

Before we begin, **you will be asked to first take a few minutes to do some sort of physical exercise,** being sure to only do as much as your physical health allows. This could include **walking, jogging, or bicycling.** After **fifteen to thirty minutes** (depending on your health) of exercise, **find a body of water to sit facing in quiet contemplation.** This can be a pond, a river, a lake, or a pool. If there are no appropriate bodies of water, light a candle and meditate while focusing on the flickering flame.

When you are seated and ready, **begin to contemplate the idea of something having no beginning and no end.** Start by visualizing a point. Now visualize a second point and a line that joins the two points into a line. Now visualize that line extending outward; now keep visualizing that line extending farther and farther outward. How far will it go if it has no end? And what if it has no beginning? Where would the start and end point of this infinite line be? Take several moments to conceptualize this notion.

Now visualize the universe with all of its untold billions of galaxies. Try and visualize it as if you're sitting in a planetarium with the vastness of all those billions of galaxies projected on the screen in front of you. Now visualize yourself flying through this infinite vastness; **attempt to visualize what the end boundary of this infinite expanse may look like. Where does it end? Where does it begin? Take several minutes to contemplate this notion of a "universe with no beginning and no end."**

When you're done, sit for several more moments and become aware of how you feel. Now look around you; do you "experience" things any differently? **Feel free to write down any of these initial thoughts and feelings,** as writing these down will help you to process this experience.

12

Good Vibrations:
Pythagoras and the Big Beat

A true mystic can break through the illusion of appearance and experience *beneath-the-surface* reality. And Pythagoras was just such a mystic. He had been able to pull back the veil and look past the façade of the physical world, where he discovered the underlying principles or structures of reality. Like a boy taking apart a watch, he was able to perceive the cogs and gears that made the watch tick.

What Pythagoras discovered was that the language of this implicate, unseen order of the universe was mathematics—the transcendent set of principles that could explain the relationship and structure of the innermost workings of the universe. The underlying level of reality couldn't be seen by the human eye, but it was accessible to the mind and intelligible to the human intellect via the transcendent principles of mathematics. Thus, mathematics not only made the universe tick, but also was—is—the language of God. Math is, in effect, the operating software of cosmic existence.

But as I've already mentioned, Pythagoras's idea of mathematics was very different from ours.

For example, what do you think of when I say the number one? Or two? Or three? We tend to view numbers as ways to quantify, or count, things. But for Pythagoras *numbers* were a living, qualitative reality that had to be approached experientially. Where we use numbers to represent *things*, for Pythagoras, numbers were *universal principles*.

Because Pythagoras also believed that science possessed a sacred dimension—a notion that would be considered quite radical today—numbers were not only seen as universal principles, but *divine* ones as well. And it was through the understanding of the universal principles of numbers that one could begin to understand—indeed, to *conceptualize*—the unity of the universe.

So, for example, one was not just a number (and not just "the loneliest number," thank you very much, Three Dog Night); instead, one represented the monad, or unity. Thus, one represented the principle of unity and the causal source from which all things arose. In that relational sense, the idea of two, the dyad, represented duality, the emergence of subject and object, and the beginning of multiplicity. Are you beginning to see how this works?

Multiplicity for Pythagoras was the beginning of strife, the tension between two objects (as many a husband or wife would agree). Yet it was also the possibility of *logos*, the Greek concept of the relation of one thing to another. (Some have compared the Greek *logos* to the Asian idea of the Tao and the tension between two objects to yin and yang.)

And what about the number three? What was behind the relational idea of three, the triad? With the advent of the triad, the gulf of dualism was bridged through the joining together of the two extremes by the third in *harmonia*—harmony.

And harmony was very important to Pythagoras.

He believed that these universal ideas or concepts could be expressed musically. By sitting around and strumming on a lyre (the ancient Greek equivalent of a guitar), he discovered the interplay

How Plato and Pythagoras Can Save Your Life

between ratios and harmonic frequency. He was able to figure out that if you half the length of a string, it would produce a note that was one octave higher. Today, in music theory classes, the mad, mystical Pythagoras is credited with having developed the theory of musical scales.

But Pythagoras went further.

He believed that these musical, mathematical, vibrational aspects weren't just limited to his lyre, but represented the essence of how the entire universe operated. In turn, he developed what has come to be called the Music of the Spheres, which is his description of the "cosmic harmony" of the universe.

This idea that the whole universe has a vibrational, mathematical, and, indeed, a musical aspect is not too far afield from modern super-string theory. As physicist Brian Greene, credited as one of the founders of super-string theory and author of the best-selling *Elegant Universe* (2004) describes it: "According to superstring theory, every particle is composed of a tiny filament of energy . . . which is shaped like a little string. And just as a violin string can vibrate in different patterns, each of which produces different musical tone, the filaments of superstring theory can also vibrate in different patterns."

It seems that Pythagoras was on to something.

But as I asked before, how did this old philosopher—without the benefit of any modern equipment, such as computers, telescopes, or electron microscopes, but just sitting in a cave in ancient Greece over twenty-five hundred years ago—somehow intuit a sense of the universe that is very much in agreement with the discoveries of our most brilliant modern theoretical physicists?

Well, I'll tell you how Pythagoras believed that he did it. He believed that through his *Bios Pythagorikos*, individuals could purify themselves—in effect, retune themselves in order to be more in alignment with this universal harmony. If individuals were "in tune," then they were healthy, happy, and balanced, since they were aligned properly with the Big Universal Harmony. And when one was aligned with the big beat of the cosmic harmony and had achieved what the mystics called mystical union (enlightenment), well, then, that's where all the answers live. Some Zen sticklers might chime in that there are no answers because there are no questions in that realm, but the point is, one would become one with (and thus aware of) *everything*.

As I've mentioned, Pythagoras claimed that he was actually able to hear this universal vibration—literally. He compared those of us unable to hear the universal vibration to blacksmiths in a noisy shop, where the loud clanging of metal interfered with the blacksmith's ability to hear anything else. If we could quiet the clanging, we could hear all sorts of other things, including the universe itself. I guess you could say that Pythagoras's idea of tuning into the universe was similar to what yogis or Buddhist monks say they're able to do through mediation—stop the chatter of their minds and thus become attuned to the universe or to the minute functioning of their own cells.

Some might find all this shocking to hear, because when most people hear "Greek philosophy," they think of logic and reason. All of this stuff about hearing the universe vibrating and contemplations on music—well, it all sounds "illogical," to quote our old friend Mr. Spock. But it wasn't so much illogical, or even irrational, as it was *beyond* logical and *beyond* rational.

Adding to the wacky fun, Pythagoras also strongly believed in *metempsychoses*, or the "transmigration of souls." That's reincarnation to you and me. Not only did he *believe* in it, but he was allegedly able to vividly recall past lives and felt that the develop-

How Plato and Pythagoras Can Save Your Life

ment of a strong memory was critically important so that a person could recall the lessons learned from past lives (see "Old-School Holistic: *The Bios Pythagorikos*" in chapter 10). It's this belief in reincarnation that's believed to have played an important role in his rather strict dietary prescriptions of semivegetarianism and his taboo against eating beans.

Beans? Semivegetarianism? I know, I know, I've got some 'splaining to do. Being a semivegetarian meant that Pythagoreans rarely ate meat, and when they did, it was usually related to a sacrificial ritual, in which case there were prescriptions against eating certain parts of the sacrificed animal. Sure, it might seem a little contradictory to not kill animals due to a belief in reincarnation while then slaughtering the occasional lamb or goat on the sacrificial altar. But hey, religion, philosophy, and science were all intertwined back in those days; occasionally, those strange bedfellows would make for odd and inbred outcomes like animal-sacrificing vegetarians. Cosmically aware metaphysicians or not, the Pythagoreans still had to offer the Olympic gods their sacrificial props once in a while.

Even though I think that most people today get the reasons behind the vegetarianism (although the sacrificial thing might be a bit of a stretch), the bean prohibition might raise a few eyebrows. I mean, really, what's the harm in eating a few beans, one might justifiably ask? Well, according to Pythagoras's brand of reincarnation, beans sometimes have the life force as well, so eating them was a no-no.

Some historians have also speculated that perhaps Pythagoras was anti-bean for health reasons. This might be a valid explanation, since Pythagoras was consumed (no gastronomical pun intended) with dietary habits that helped keep a person clear-headed and alert. Indeed, it was for those clear-headed reasons that he was opposed to drinking alcohol or eating foods that could make one sluggish. So in addition to perceiving beans as soul-bearing vessels, given Pythagoras's emphasis on a healthy diet, it's possible that he was anti-bean because of beans, um, rather gaseous gastronomical effects, which can make people sluggish and less than nimble on their feet.

Most historians have attributed these reincarnation and dietary beliefs to Pythagoras's time spent traveling and studying in Egypt and Babylon. One can easily see in many of the Pythagorean customs the ways of the ancient Egyptians and Babylonians, including their belief in reincarnation, their refusal to eat beans, and their belief in the purification of the soul through rigorous intellectual and ethical practices.

While it's quite plausible that Pythagoras did indeed absorb these exotic esoteric beliefs during his many travels, he shaped these ideas and beliefs into a system that would become distinctly his own. And this distinctly flavored *Pythagoreanism* would, in turn, greatly influence one of the most important people that have ever walked the earth: Plato.

Exercise 9

The Cosmic Symphony:
Music from the Universal Orchestra

This contemplative exercise deals with the **Music of the Spheres, Pythagoras's notion that the vibrational aspect of the universe actually created a form of cosmic music.** For this exercise, you will be asked to go to the website "World Science" (*www.world-science.net),* which features information about **asteroseismology,** a branch of astronomy that actually detects and records the **imperceptible-to-the-human-ear "music" that various stars or galactic bodies make.**

Astronomer Donald Kurtz from the University of Central Lancashire in Preston, U.K., explains how during the 1970s, astronomers discovered that **"the sun and other stars do actually 'sing.'"** According to Kurtz, **stars produce a ghostly whistling, drumming, humming, or rumbling sound** through their frequencies, or speeds of vibration, but those sounds must be artificially boosted to bring them into human hearing range.

"Stars have natural vibrations that are sound waves, just as musical instruments do," Kurtz explains. "In the case of an instrument such as a horn, the cause of the vibrations is the musician blowing on the horn and buzzing his or her lips at a frequency that matches the natural vibrations of the horn. For the star, the vibrations start by changes in the passage of energy from the nuclear inferno in the heart of the star on its way to the surface, and escape into space."

In 2005, researchers published a paper noting that **a massive quake had left a neutron star vibrating like a bell, creating a note corresponding to what we would designate as F sharp.** Early in 2006, scientists reported that not only do stars vibrate musically, but **the entire Milky Way is also oscillating in a manner very similar to a drumhead.**

For this meditation, you must first go to the website "World Science," *(www.world-science.net/othernews/060809_spheres.htm)*, and listen to the first three *very brief* (only several seconds each) **asteroseismological downloads** produced by the website and England's Sheffield Hallam University. If, for any reason, you cannot access this website, do a Google search for "astereseismology" and access any available downloads of interstellar sounds. If it is not possible to find asteroseismological music, then simply listen to any gently rhythmic or repeating music (tribal or New Age can work well).

If you have been able to access the "World Science" website: The first download is a recording of **HR3831, a new class of star with a powerful magnetic field that pulses every 11.7 minutes.** The second is a recording of **Xi-hydrae, an old star in the constellation Hydra that creates a sound very reminiscent of African drumming**. The third recording is of **a "dead" white dwarf star fifty light years away from earth, in Centaurus.**

Next, sit in quiet, meditative repose, as you have done in the earlier contemplations, while you play the final download, called *Stellar Music No. 1* by Jenő Keuler and Zoltán Kolláth. It is the first piece of music ever composed for stellar instruments. (If you have not been able to access the "World Science" stellar music, then play whatever rhythmic music you were able to obtain.)

As you listen to this galactic music, try and visualize—or, more appropriately, try **and *experience*—the vibration of the music of the spheres**. As you sit and become aware of the music, **try to use your higher mind to visualize or conceptualize the music as the infinitesimal vibrations of string theory described by Brian Greene.**

As you continue to listen to this cosmic symphony, **try and listen or feel the harmony and vibration within your own body. Feel the vibrations of the body's tens of billions of cells, which are comprised of an almost infinite number of atoms that are themselves comprised of tiny**

How Plato and Pythagoras Can Save Your Life

vibrating little filaments, all coming together to create the symphony that is uniquely you.

Next, turn your attention outwards. As the music continues to play, try and actually **feel the vibration of not only your own being, but also of the entire universe.** Try, in fact, to **entrain these two frequencies**—that is, **try and attune your own vibration with that of the larger cosmic rhythm.**

When you're done, sit for several more moments and become aware of how you feel. Now look around the room again; do you experience it any differently? **Feel free to write down any of these initial thoughts and feelings,** as writing them down will help you to process this experience.

PART FIVE

Escaping Plato's Cave

May not you and I be confluent in a higher consciousness
and confluently active there, though we now know it not?
We finite minds may simultaneously be co-conscious
with one another in a super-human intelligence.

—William James

All of life is a near-death experience.

—Alan Harris

Part of our psyche is not in time and not in space. They are only
an illusion, time and space, and so in a certain part
of our psyche time does not exist at all.

—Carl Jung

13

Plato's Retreat—
from the Material World

The legendary British philosopher Lord Whitehead once said that all of philosophy was just a series of footnotes to Plato. Indeed, much of Western civilization stands on his broad shoulders. (By the way, the Greek word *platon* means "broad-backed one," which the handsome and aristocratic Plato was alleged to have been as a youth.)

If Western civilization is standing on Plato's shoulders, it might be fair to say that Plato is, in turn, standing—and straddling—on Socrates and Pythagoras's deltoids (can't get away from Pythagoras and those triangles!), as he was greatly influenced by each of their distinct philosophies. That's a very important point to make regarding Plato, who seems to have two phases in his life. In fact, it can be said that there was Plato, the early years, when he paid tribute to Socrates and his concerns about the human condition, and Plato, the sunset years, when we see a more metaphysical, cosmologically interested Plato. Georgetown professor Daniel Robinson has described this evolution in Plato's orientation as a shift from "anthropos to cosmos." According to some accounts, this shift is alleged to have occurred as a result of Plato spending time with a community of Pythagoreans in western Greece after the death of his beloved teacher, Socrates.

To many, Plato *is* Greek philosophy. As the student of Socrates and the teacher of Aristotle, he shaped ancient Greek philosophy and, subsequently, all of Western thought like no other human being who has ever lived.

Plato would go on to develop his theory of *Forms*, which built upon not only Socrates' ideas of absolute and abstract properties, but also upon Pythagoras's theories of pure and transcendent numbers, as well as Parmenides' notion of an eternal and unchanging reality (more about that later). And it was Plato's notion of an eternal soul that would create the framework for a theological revolution that would shape early Christianity, change biblical Judaism into rabbinic Judaism, and greatly impact Islam as well.

Plato's radical and unheard of notion of an immaterial soul that was separate from the physical body (in fact, not only was it considered separate, but Plato saw it as being trapped by the physical body, as a bird is trapped in a cage) would necessitate that Judaism, Christianity, and Islam create a place to put this pesky, eternal soul. Voila! Enter a belief in "the world to come" (*olam ha'bah* in Hebrew), which Christians and Muslims conceptualize as heaven (or, for the sinners in the room, a not-very-pleasant hell).

Plato himself never spoke of heaven and hell. What we know of his view of the soul's afterlife is described in the myth of Er, found in Plato's *Republic*. Here, Plato tells the story of a soldier, Er, who dies in battle, but is revived on his funeral pyre and then is able to describe what happens after check-out time. Er describes a rather karmic-inspired conception of a reincarnation-driven afterlife, a place where the good are rewarded with the choice of their next life and the truly despicable (whom he describes as murderers and tyrants) are permanently stuck down under. Once a new life is assigned, the soul travels to the Plain of Oblivion and has to drink from the River Lethe (the River of Forgetfulness), which makes the soul unable to remember anything from the prior incarnation.

Christianity, Judaism, and Islam weren't really that interested in Plato's view (or Pythagoras's for that matter) of reincarnation and the transmigration of souls; rather, it was Plato's notion that the soul and body were not one and the same that the religiously inclined picked up on.

This Greek metaphysical conception of matter and spirit—of body as separate from soul—was first introduced to the Judaic Pharisees (later called rabbis) in 331 BCE by Alexander the Great, who was himself a student of Aristotle. Before that time, the Hebrew Bible never *mentions* any type of life after death or form of soul survival; the closest thing it comes to is in describing a Hades-like place of the dead, called *Sheol*. Pre–Alexander the Great, the belief in Judaism had been that when life (*nefesh*) ended, that was it. It wasn't until the infusion of Greek philosophy and the platonic notion of a separate soul that Judaism distinguished what came to be called rabbinic Judaism from biblical Judaism.

For the Christians, it was first St. Augustine, during the fourth century, and later Thomas Aquinas, during the medieval period, that helped to infuse platonism as essential doctrine in Christianity.

After Judaism, Christianity, and Islam were exposed to Plato's concept of a transcendent realm beyond the physical—and that the human soul was a card-carrying member of this realm—well then, happy day! The soul was born and, with it, the notion of spiritual immortality. Thank you, Plato, for eternal life! Yet these were all much-later theological interpretations of a greater platonic notion that attempted to explain the relationship between the physical world with a transcendent, non-corporal realm that Plato had called the Realm of Forms or Realm of Ideas.

In Plato's view of reality, what we perceived as the "real," or material, world might, in fact, just be smoke and mirrors; indeed, the physical world accessible to our senses may just be shadows of this higher Ideal Realm. The only things that Plato believed to be real were, by definition, eternal. Since the physical world was strictly ephemeral—as fleeting as the grains of sand spilling through the hourglass—and had no permanence, it *couldn't* be real.

But what *was* real were the Eternal Forms—those transcendent and pure Ideas that existed on a plane beyond space and time. What our senses were able to perceive here on our earthly plane were just the aforementioned shadows the imperfect *copies* or illusions of the real, Eternal Forms.

A quick example: a basketball is a scuffed and imperfect physical copy of the pure and Ideal Form of a sphere, which is eternal and perfect and exists independent of human thought and perception; the NBA just happens to make crude and imperfect rubber knock-offs of that perfect Form.

Similarly, even the Ideal Form for something a little more abstract—like, say, beauty or courage—was not a subjective, culturally specific *definition* of the word. Rather, it was a universal truth that actually existed in a beyond-corporeal realm and that could become *imperfectly* manifest in the physical realm (like the scuffed basketball).

Plato shared the Pythagorean view that the intellect could unlock the door of this transcendent realm. Like Pythagoras, he

How Plato and Pythagoras Can Save Your Life

believed that contemplation, as a meditative practice in which the objects of contemplation are mathematics, cosmology, ethics, logic riddles, and the nature of life and death, could expand a person's consciousness and level of awareness. Indeed, written over the door of Plato's famous Academy, considered by many to be the first college, was the inscription, "Let no one enter here who is ignorant of mathematics." Mathematics for Plato, as for Pythagoras, was a very powerful tool to elevate a person's consciousness.

Consciousness expansion was the name of the game for the metaphysically inclined mystic philosophers. But in order for that expansion to happen, one had to get past the illusion of the senses; this overreliance on the senses could be a mystical dealbreaker when it came to experiencing the beyond-sensory Ideal Realm. Plato even discussed this sensory trap in his most famous allegory, the "Myth of the Cave" (see "Plato's Funky Cave"). And it wasn't just our senses that were a potential trap; for the Greek mystics, an overreliance on reason and logic could also trip up people as they attempted to experience mystical union. While the ancient Greeks believed that a reasoning mind *can* indeed be a key to help unlock the door of our transcendent awareness, they also felt that that same key could also close that door by tricking our minds into believing that the illusion of our sensory world—the illusion that Plato warned against in his "Myth of the Cave"—is *all* that there is to reality.

As noted earlier, in Hinduism there's the analogous concept of *Maya*, which is confusing the sensory world with Ultimate Reality. In jnana yoga, there's a very close parallel to the Greek concept of using reason as a key to unlock the door of our higher mind in order to transcend sensory illusion.

Plato's Funky Cave

Plato's most famous passage in all of his writings occurs in the *Republic* and has come to be known as "the Myth of the Cave." This story symbolically conveys Plato's view on reality, knowledge, and human perception.

In this allegory, Plato describes a large cave cut off from the outside world by a long passage that prevents any sunlight from entering the cave. And in this deep, dark place we find a row of prisoners, who are chained by their limbs and necks so that they can't move. They can't even turn their heads to the left or right and see the prisoners next to them. All that they can see is the wall of the cave directly facing them.

To make matters worse for our poor misbegotten inmates, they have *always* been chained up like that; they have never known anything else. (Hey, that's why it's called a myth!) The only source of light is a bright fire in the cave behind them. And unknown to them, there's also a rampart behind them, on which people are perpetually passing back and forth, carrying things on the prisoners' heads. Our cave-dwelling prisoners can't see these people, nor can the prisoners directly hear them. All that they can see are the people's shadows produced by the light of the fire in the wall facing the prisoners, and all they can hear is the echo of the people's voices bouncing off of that same wall. So all the poor buggers have ever experienced in their entire lives are those shadows and echoes; to them, that's reality, because that all that their senses have ever revealed to them.

continued

How Plato and Pythagoras Can Save Your Life

Plato writes that if one of the prisoners were to attempt to break free and escape, *Shawshank Redemption* style, he would initially be confused and disoriented. When he turns around and sees the fire, the flames would at first dazzle his eyes. He might even be inclined to want to forget the whole thing, sit up straight, and just go back to the safety and comfort of looking straight ahead at the shadows. And if our rebel were to break out of the cave entirely, the blazing sunlight would temporarily blind and confuse him even more than the fire did, and it might be a long time before he understood anything.

Eventually, he'd acclimate.

But then if he were to once again return to that dark cave, he'd be temporarily blinded once again, only this time by the darkness. And if he'd tried to describe what he'd seen to his former fellow prisoners, who were still shackled and chained and still only knowing the shadows, they'd think he was crazy. "Brothers, I've seen the light—literally! What you think is real isn't! It's just bloody shadows on the wall!" he'd scream. But they wouldn't know what he was talking about; they'd think he was nuts.

It's a pretty powerful allegory. Clearly Plato's view was that human beings were shackled inside the prison of their bodies and that knowledge was mediated by the limitations of our senses. In his view, the true essence of reality goes way beyond the sensible (as in the five senses), which can detect only the illusory shadows of a deeper reality.

Most people tend to think of yoga as a physical practice; indeed, yoga studios of all shapes and flavors have exploded on the American workout scene. But yoga was—and is—really more than just about burning calories or developing muscle tone.

The word *yoga* is derived from the Sanskrit and literally means "to yoke." The idea is that the individual soul is yoked to the Hindu notion of *Brahman*, otherwise known as the Ultimate or Eternal Reality, which is analogous to Plato's Ideal Realm or Pythagoras's Informational Realm. (Pythagoras's ideas that a noncorporeal realm of Pure Number—Informational Realm—was thought to have inspired Plato's Ideal Realm of Eternal Forms.) For the yoga practitioner, the adherence to one of the five major yoga paths can lead to *Moksha*, which is a release from the earthly bonds of illusion; like Plato's allegorical cave dweller, those who achieve *Moksha* escape from *Maya*, the belief that the cave of illusion and shadows is all there is to reality.

The five yoga paths are bhakti yoga, the path of devotion or selfless love; karma yoga, the path of action, deeds, and service; hatha yoga, the way of bodily or physical development; raja yoga, also known as contemplative yoga, which uses meditation to achieve liberation; and finally, jnana yoga, the way of the intellect or knowledge. While *jnana* literally translates to "knowledge" in Sanskrit, it's generally believed to mean knowledge of the *true self*, because, as Hindus believe, to merge and *yoke* with Brahman is jnana—knowledge of the true self.

Plato outlived his teacher, Socrates, by fifty years. During that time, he wrote approximately twenty-four dialogues wherein the protagonist was always Socrates. And although he would be best known for his theory of Eternal Forms, he never presents a systematic explication of this theory in his writings. Instead, expositions, discussions, and critical examinations occur in a number of his dialogues, giving the reader a sense of the flavor of what Plato came to believe regarding the Forms.

What is quite clear about Plato is that he took the death of his beloved teacher very hard. Socrates was a short, pug-nosed, yet charismatic philosopher who had developed a question-and-answer approach known as *elenchus*, which was meant to stimulate a reexamination of one's beliefs towards a deeper and fuller understanding of what one thinks that they know. This technique came to be known as the *Socratic Method* and eventually gave rise to the *dialectic*. Socrates believed that it was critically important to question everything. But when Socrates would ask a question like "What is justice?" he was looking for people to examine the common and abstract property called justice.

Socrates' deep and enduring interest was in human affairs, where he valued personal and moral integrity above everything else—even his own life. At the time of Socrates' death (while his student Plato was still a relatively young man), there had been much political upheaval and unrest in Athens, which was at war with neighboring Sparta. When a new regime—a regime that was partly comprised of Plato's influential family—took power in Athens, Socrates was charged with not worshiping the gods of the state, introducing unfamiliar religious practices, and corrupting the young Athenians with what were labeled his rather subversive ideas. If he were found guilty of those charges, the penalty would be death.

Here's where Socrates demonstrated that his personal integrity meant more to him than his own life. It was assumed that he would simply exile himself, as was the prevailing custom, and thus avoid the trial and his potential date with the Grim Reaper. But

Socrates insisted that to exile himself would go against his sense of duty and his principle of abiding by whatever Athens decreed. He chose to stand trial and conducted his own defense. He was found guilty and sentenced to death.

Even then, he did not take an opportunity to avoid death. During the month that elapsed between his sentencing and his expected execution, his friends arranged for him to escape and thus save himself. But he refused.

He spent the last day of his life discussing philosophy, having a very timely discussion with his two close friends, Cebes and Timias, about the immortality of the soul before drinking his hemlock.

Plato took his death very hard. As a still-young man of thirty, he decided to leave Athens and traveled with several other followers of Socrates to Egypt and then Sicily, where it's believed that he encountered the Pythagoreans. Upon returning to Athens, he formed his legendary school, the Academy, where he continued to teach and write his dialogues until his death at the age of eighty-four. The Academy would remain a beacon of philosophical learning for several hundred years after Plato's death, until it was finally closed in 524 CE by Justinian I of Byzantium, who had feared that it was a threat to the propagation of Christianity.

While Plato is much better known than his predecessor Pythagoras, he's not deified or imbued with superhuman abilities as Pythagoras is. Perhaps this is a result of his prolific writing; since Pythagoras and Socrates themselves never wrote anything, it would seem that that vacuum was filled by mythic exaggeration.

How Plato and Pythagoras Can Save Your Life

Or, perhaps, Pythagoras *was* more the supranormal mystic than Plato was. Indeed, some have viewed Plato's approach as more *intellectual* than experiential because it meant acquiring an intellectual grasp of the eternal realm of Ideal Forms, while Pythagoras and the other, more hard-core mystics strove for mystical union—the trippy merging of the Self with the infinite.

It is true that Plato seemed comfortable with philosophical discourse, and, indeed, all of his written works were written in the form of dialogues (always between Socrates and a variety of other characters). But Plato himself did come to regard the Ideal Forms as divine, and he did have a theological conception of a *deimurge* ("creator"), or what Aristotle later called the "Unmoved Mover" (the animating cause of motion that is itself beyond movement, beyond space, and beyond time).

Although the bulk of Plato's philosophical influence has been on thinkers who are irreligious and decline to ascribe any divine interpretation to his philosophy, their view does not see the man and his beliefs for what they were and seems to project on Plato a secularism that contradicts his theistic orientation.

A topic that obsessed Pythagoras, Plato, Heraclitus, and Parmenides was the question of change. This question was actually a larger philosophical exploration into the nature of being versus becoming. And part of that philosophical journey centered around the notion of physical death or what Plato had indicated was the goal of philosophical purification: freeing the soul from the shackles of the body. Plato even said that the ultimate goal of philosophy was "death before dying."

Huh? Dying? What's dying got to do with this?

Maybe everything.

But before you start thinking that I'm advocating speed dialing Dr. Kevorkian and his magic deep-sleep machine, let me explain.

Pythagoras, Plato, Parmenides, Plotinus—they all embraced life. But they also realized that to truly experience Ultimate Reality, the road there would have to lead through self-annihilation. But *physical* death is a pretty final gambit; there's no coming back if you're wrong. I keep thinking of those Nike-wearing Heaven's Gate cultists in the 1990s who killed themselves so they could ride in the tail of the Hale-Bopp comet. It's a pretty ballsy move. But perhaps there's some other way to "die before dying," so that a person doesn't have to do it the old-school flat-lining way, like I did, or by drinking the Jim Jones Kool-Aid.

Sure enough, the Greeks *did* discover a way to die before dying. It involved going underground—deep, deep, underground, into the cold darkness of a cave.

Exercise 10

The Universe as One Big Thought

This contemplative exercise deals with the **Plato's Ideal Forms.**

The British mathematician and physicist Sir James Jeans remarked that, as a result of the new discoveries in science, **"The Universe begins to look more like a great thought than a great machine."** In this chapter about Plato, we see that he too felt that an immaterial, thoughtlike **Ideal Realm was primary in our universe over an imperfect physical world, which he viewed as a shadow of that Ideal Realm.**

But before we begin, **take a few minutes to do some sort of physical exercise,** being sure to only do as much as your physical health allows. This could include **walking, jogging, or bicycling.** After **fifteen to thirty minutes** (depending on your health) of exercise, **find a body of water to sit facing in quiet contemplation.** This can be a pond, a river, a lake, or a pool. If there are no appropriate bodies of water, light a candle and meditate while focusing on the flickering flame.

As you begin your contemplation, **ponder the implications of Einstein's theory of relativity, which says matter (the physical) is just dense, compact energy (thought). What if the universe is indeed a great thought (as Sir Jeans speculated) and the material world is just a manifestation of those thoughts from the Ideal Realm?** Take several minutes to contemplate these ideas.

Finally, **contemplate the Ideal Form of a sphere. Has that Form always existed?** **Can a basketball come into existence if that Form did not exist?** Take a few more minutes to contemplate this question.

When you're done, sit for several more moments and become aware of how you feel. Now look around you; do you experience things any differently? **Feel free to write down any of these initial thoughts and feelings,** as writing these down will help you to process this experience.

14

On the Nature of Change:
The More Things Change . . .

The question regarding the nature of change haunts me.

Even while I acknowledge that I've changed so many things about my life, the question of whether or not I've *really* changed still eats at me. Sure, I've had my own personal alchemy and have transformed from the addicted nightclub owner that I used to be into the different—better—person that I feel that I am today. But have I *really* changed?

All this self-reflection leads me to wonder if anyone ever *really* changes? And here I'm talking about real, who-we-are-at-our-essence-type of change, not merely modifying or altering undesirables behaviors or lifestyles, like quitting smoking or becoming a vegetarian. My god, in my professional life I work with recovering addicts every day who have changed so many of their problematic behaviors. But have *they* changed?

I guess what I'm asking is whether or not we can, in effect, change the DNA of our soul.

I mean, after all, even if the proverbial leopard could change its spots or a tiger its stripes, underneath it all, aren't they still the same predators? When a caterpillar transforms into a butterfly, isn't it still at its core what it was before the wings sprouted? A block of ice melts into a puddle of water, but isn't it still two parts hydrogen and one part oxygen? Of course it may look different, but is the ice so really different from that messy puddle?

The ancient Greek philosophers had opposing views on this question of change, both personal and cosmological. Heraclitus was all about change. He believed that reality, at its essence, was constantly in flux, a dynamic force akin to fire that could never remain static. He once famously said that one can never step into the same river twice because the river, ever fluid, was never, moment-to-moment, the same river. Taken to the personal level, Heraclitus's principle means an individual is never the same person from moment-to-moment. Ask yourself if you are exactly the same person that you were a few seconds ago before you started reading this page. In fact, some Buddhists have a similar notion: that a person is reincarnating into a new entity from each moment to the next.

But yet another Greek philosopher, Parmenides thought that was nonsense. He and his student Zeno believed that what we think is change is mere illusion; it's merely the *appearance* of change. Fundamentally, the universe has a totality or a wholeness to it that's unchanging. In fact, Zeno came up with his clever little logic-paradox riddles to illustrate the point that change is merely a trick of the mind (see "Logic Paradoxes: Achilles and the Tortoise" in chapter 9).

An analogous Buddhist view regarding this *appearance* of superficial change versus one's non-changing essence is the metaphor of the candle. Unlike Heraclitus's perspective of fire as dynamic change, the Buddhists' view is that the fire of a candle symbolizes static continuity, the unchanging aspect of the candle. In their conception, a candle flame contains the true essence of the candle; once all the wick and wax has been nearly used up, the flame can be "reincarnated" into a new physical manifestation by the lighting of a new candle. The new candle may look different from the old one; the flame may be "clothed" differently, or it may now be in a different body, to use anthropocentric language, but the essence of the candle has not changed. The flame is the same flame.

Think here of the Olympic torch ceremony. Great effort and pains are taken to carry—and pass—from runner to runner, the same flame all the way around the world. Runners and torches may change, but that good old flame is still the same flame.

So the question begs repeating: can people ever truly change? Are we, like Heraclitus's dynamic fire, changing from moment-to-moment, or are we, at essence, the same unchanging candle flame as it is passed along from moment-to-moment and candle-to-candle?

I believe that the answer lays in mystical paradox: human beings are simultaneously static and dynamic. We are in flux, yet that change is part of the unchanging whole. We are different incarnations from moment-to-moment, like Heraclitus's dynamic fire, yet we are also the same energetic essence, just as in the candle flame.

Put into human terms, we are essentially who we were when we were seven-year-old children telling our parents what we wanted to be when we grew up, and yet we are also different, in some very real sense, from the person that we were ten seconds ago when we started reading this page.

Adding another deeper and subtler distinction regarding the nature of reality, let me go back to the ancient Greeks, Buddhists, and other metaphysicians for a moment. In their non-dual (often called monistic) conceptions of reality, not only change, but also separateness (the belief that there is a separation or a dualism between things) is viewed as illusion.

The stereotypical Buddhist view of "all is one" reflects this profound idea that everything is a part of the universal totality. This includes people, planets, thoughts—everything. That's not to reductionistically say that everything *is* the same, but rather that everything is part of the cosmic soup, just as carrots are different from celery chunks, but they're both part of the total *allness* that comprises my chicken soup.

Some quantum physicists argue that the carrots and the celery *are* the same, since they are fundamentally made up of the same subatomic building blocks known as quanta, and just *appear* to be different because they assume different properties depending on their vibrational "frequencies" (more about this in chapter 15). In these quantum-physics conceptions, what we perceive as matter is really just dense information. This conception is shared by several extremely smart and rigorously trained academics, like physicist Amit Goswami, author of *The Self-Aware Universe* (2005), and Ervin Laszlo, author of *Science and the Akashic Field*. Both have suggested that perhaps this causal informational realm is what others have called universal or cosmic consciousness, or what Plato called the Ideal Realm.

Mystics, as well as some scientists, believe that our soul essence, or what some may more secularly call consciousness, is not an epiphenomenon of (that is, a phenomenon caused by and dependent on) the biological computer that we call a brain. Some modern theoreticians have speculated that perhaps instead of consciousness being an epiphenomenon of matter vis-à-vis the brain, perhaps it is the other way around; perhaps, as Plato suggests, matter and the entire physical universe are an epiphenomenon of consciousness.

In my conception, weaned from academic investigation, as well as mystical insights, the universe is indeed informational and vibrational. It is also, in its infinite totality, what some may call

God, and it is unfolding with a complexity and purpose that is, perhaps, beyond our ability to comprehend.

Eminent MIT theologian Huston Smith once said at a conference that I attended that we, as human beings, can't appreciate the numinous, or what he called "the infinite," because we are finite creatures with finite brains, and thus, "the finite container cannot contain the infinite." Others have argued that we do indeed touch the infinite, because we are the infinite. In some of these conceptions, individual human consciousness is a raindrop in the greater ocean of consciousness.

And as has been mentioned, there is the mystical belief that we are one with the divine (monism)—that is, everything *is* God or, for the more secular, the universe. My belief is that we contain part of the infinite essence and are hardwired in an evolutionary way towards a deeper, greater mystical unfolding, just as the universe, too, is unfolding. Thus, we seek mystical union because it's hardwired into our spiritual DNA.

It is truly amazing to consider that the entire universe, with all its billions of galaxies, was, at the original point of the Big Bang, known as "the singularity"—no more than a subatomic cosmic speck. It is perhaps, as Huston Smith suggested, "unimaginable" that from that speck of invisible dust 15 billion years ago, the universe would infinitely unfold and evolve in such a way that self-aware sentient beings would be able to look back and self-reflect on the nature and origin of the universe that not only created them, but embodies them as well.

Perhaps, as some have suggested, we are made of the elemental cosmic dust of the universe, and thus, we *are* the universe trying to not only *experience*, but to also *understand* itself.

Perhaps sentient beings are the universe's neurons, ever evolving to form larger, more interconnected neural networks that represent the consciousness of the universe, or the universal Mind. As in holograms, as well as in cellular life, where every smaller part contains all the information of the larger whole, not only do we seem to be neurons in the universal Mind, but we also seem to posses within us, imprinted in something akin to spiritual DNA, the key to the larger mysteries of the entire universal brain.

Yet to access the mysteries of that larger numinous realm, the Ancient Greeks felt that one needed to cross into the underworld and experience death. This ancient tradition, rooted in Orphism (the ancient Greek "mystery school" that honored both Persephone and the mythic poet Orpheus, both of whom were said to have ventured to the "underworld" and returned), also required a journey into the darkness. But why was this journey necessary?

Exercise 11

Change: The Great Illusion

The exercise deals with the nature of **change.**

Before we begin, **take a few minutes to do some sort of physical exercise,** being sure to only do as much as your physical health allows. This could include **walking, jogging, or bicycling.** After **fifteen to thirty minutes** (depending on your health), **find a body of water to sit facing in quiet contemplation.** This can be a pond, a river, a lake, or a pool. If there are no appropriate bodies of water, light a candle and meditate while focusing on the flickering flame.

When you are seated and ready to begin, **take a deep breath** and reflect on **whether or not you are the same person that woke up this morning.** Are you exactly the same, **or are you any different?**

Now try and **contemplate whether you are the same person you were when you were a ten-year-old.** Do you feel that you are still essentially that same child looking through the same pair of eyes, **or have you fundamentally changed?**

Now ask yourself this question**: is the flame that gets passed on to another torch still the same flame, or is it different?**

Now **visualize the entire universe with all of its billions of galaxies.** As impossible as it is to conceive, **try and conceptualize the time of the Big Bang, when the untold mass of the universe was contained in a super-dense subatomic speck. Is it still the same universe, or has it changed?**

Finally, **contemplate time. Is it moving** or changing, **or are you merely experiencing movement as you accumulate experiences?**

When you're done, sit for several more moments and become aware of how you feel. Now look around you; do you experience things any differently? **Feel free to write down any of these initial thoughts and feelings,** as writing these down will help you to process this experience.

15

Death: The New Birth

The ancient Greeks really got into death.

From the harvest and fertility mythology that describes how an abducted Persephone gets taken into the underworld by a smitten Hades, to death-recreating Orphic mystery rites, the Greeks seemed very into the death thing.

Why? Why the morbid fascination with the underworld? Indeed, why has even philosophy itself been called by Plato a form of "death before dying"?

I'll tell you why: philosophy was all about breaking the bird (the soul) free from the cage (the physical body). Once a person was able to really experience that—that is to say, once a person was able to actually touch his or her infinite aspect, in this case via the purification of mystical philosophy, which included a death rehearsal known as an *incubation*—well, it sort of puts everything else in perspective.

Plato (as well as Pythagoras) believed that in realizing our ephemeral physical nature, we would better apprehend our transcendent and eternal soul. These sentiments—the belief that through purification, the soul is freed from the shackles of the body—are what Socrates is quoted in the *Phaedo* dialogue as saying the philosopher's primary goal should be. Plato and the other Greek mystic philosophers believed that through this combination of purification (through a lifestyle and practices like those of the *Bios Pythagorikos*) and the death rehearsals of incubations, a person could get beyond the illusion of the material world and experience what the mystics call Ultimate Reality.

Parmenides was another very prominent Greek philosopher who also greatly emphasized the importance of this technique. Who was Parmenides, you ask? Parmenides of Elea is believed by some scholars to have been a student of one of Pythagoras's students, Ameneias. There is also some speculation that Parmenides and his main disciple, Zeno, had an encounter with the young Socrates in Athens during the festival of the great *Panathanaea*. Whether there was actually any personal meeting between Pythagoras's disciples, Parmenides and Socrates, is unclear; what is apparent is that the Pythagoreans influenced Parmenides and, in turn, Parmenides' Eleatic school influenced platonic thinking.

Traditionally, Parmenides is considered by many classicists to be the "father of logic," but there's been some recent scholarly debate questioning this Mr. Spock–like version of Parmenides. After going back to original Greek version of Parmenides' writings, recent historians have emerged with a new, much more mystical version of Parmenides than one that could have hung tough with the Vulcan contingent at a *Star Trek* convention. The guy claimed to have received his insights during dreamlike altered states of consciousness in which a goddess taught him all there was to know! He used this knowledge as an *Iatromantis*—a healer who was able to receive messages directly from the gods. Does this sound logical—or even rational—by today's

How Plato and Pythagoras Can Save Your Life

standards? Father of logic? This dream-interpreting, goddess-channeling, altered-state-tripping philosopher? I don't think so.

To further confuse things, Parmenides imparted the insights from his goddess friend to others in teasingly difficult (and quite awkward) hexametric poetry. According to classical historian Peter Kingsley and his interpretation of the original Greek, the goddess in Parmenides' vision was Persephone, goddess of the underworld, and the transformative message that she imparted was the message of *dying before we die.* (There's that death thing again!)

For the Greeks of Parmenides' day, Hades wasn't just a place of darkness and death; instead, it was, as Kingsley described it, "[t]he supreme place of paradox where all the opposites meet . . . [where] the source of the light is at home in the darkness" (Kingsley, 2004).

This journey in which one faced one's own death and darkness—one's own shadow side—was part of a transformative and integrating hero's journey, to use Joseph Campbell's language, in which one could die before dying, learning to "no longer to live on the surface of yourself" (Kingsley, 1999). This process of transfiguration was the human alchemy that Carl Jung discovered and that the Greeks, Egyptians, and Babylonians had practiced thousands of years before Jung had even been born.

This was the healing—and potentially transformative—journey that Parmenides was referring to in his poetry; *this* was the technique that Pythagoras had learned in Egypt and in Babylon: the symbolic physical death of the body as part of a new spiritual rebirth.

During an incubation ritual, a person is supposed to go into a dark cave and lay totally still for hours, even days. Through this process, if individuals are properly trained and prepared, they can experience a pretty amazing physical catharsis wherein there is a sense of shedding the physical body as a snake sheds its skin. (In my case, maybe I took the death-before-dying piece a little too literally.)

Perhaps the real key to the transformation—the magic, if you will—that seems to accompany actual near-death experiences lays with the dissolution of the Self and the glimpse into the infinite. This explanation certainly borrows more from the ancient Greeks than it does from New Age, "step into the light" orientations.

In the incubation rituals of the ancient Greeks, the key was to let go of one's self. In a sense, death can be seen as a release or expansion of the individual egoic level of consciousness into the larger expanse. As the walls of the Self are torn down, what's left? Nothing? Or is that nothing perhaps everything—what some call the "allness" of existence? Is it possible that in losing our individualistic sense of a skin-wrapped self, we begin to merge into mystical union with that allness of the universe? After all, what stops us from expanding our level of consciousness to be able to apprehend the infinite?

The Greeks suggested that our senses can get in the way; our biology traps us into a single container, physiologically constraining us to being able to apprehend things only through our five sense organs. And then our culture interacts with our individual psychology as we develop habits of mind that limit the ways we can perceive and experience our world. But what if all of these biological, cultural, and psychological limitations were stripped away? What would you be left with? Some suggest all of that *needs* to be stripped away before Ultimate Reality could be apprehended.

What are some tools that can help us tear down the constraining walls of the familiar—and indeed, of our very selves?

Well, drug addiction does a pretty good job of battering the Self into nonexistence. And death has a neat way of doing that as well. In fact, in the case of an overdose, you get a twofer: the ego-destroying combo package of death and addiction! Of course, beyond death and addiction there are the less destructive and somewhat more pleasant ego-dampening techniques from the various meditation traditions.

I've come to believe that the transformative magic involved with my near-death experience lay in the way my sense of an individual identity was destroyed. Without that constraint, I experienced a sense of *unbelievable* fullness. Really, without the limitations of self, one gets a better perspective of the larger cosmological reality. And *perspective* may be too limiting of a word. When one steps into the void, one *experiences* a deeper sense of connectedness with that larger reality.

That's what I've taken away from my near-death experience. Can I prove any of this? No, not in the empirical sense. But then again, I don't feel that I have to, because, on another level, the proof is in the pudding: I *have* transformed. It's that end result that matters most to me. The transformation happened; to hell with proving to naysayers that it wasn't related to something a bit more special and transcendent than endorphin releases or some other neatly quantifiable explanation. Who cares about that?

All I know is that I traveled to the underworld and came back a different person.

Breaking Free From the Cage via Altered States: Flotation Tanks and Dr. John C. Lilly

In the 1980 film *Altered States*, William Hurt portrays a Harvard scientist who attempts to expand his consciousness and explore the depths of not only his own psyche but also of reality itself via experimentation with psychedelic drugs while immersed in a sensory-deprivation tank (a.k.a., a flotation, Samadhi, or sense-dep tank).

In the film, Hurt's character becomes dangerously obsessed with this metaphysical quest. He seems to not only lose his grip on reality, but also begins to actually genetically regress during his mind-altered sessions. He experiences traveling back towards the primordial past, and during those jaunts, where his consciousness travels across spacetime, he emerged from the tank as a hairy, knuckle-dragging cross between Big Foot and Chewbacca.

Pretty crazy stuff, right? That movie has to be fiction, doesn't it? Well, while it is fictionalized with a bit of Hollywood flair, the film actually depicts the work of a real researcher. Allow me to introduce you to Dr. John C. Lilly, the genius who first discovered some of the incredible consciousness-expanding effects of sensory-deprivation tanks (while ingesting heavy doses of at first LSD and later ketamine). Like the William Hurt character, Lilly also seemingly lost his mind as he spoke of astral travel, extraterrestrial beings, and interspecies communication (although, thankfully, he did avoid the ape-suit metamorphosis).

But was he crazy? Did he lose his mind? Just who was

continued

Lilly and what doors did his research open (albeit with many caveats) for those of us who are aspiring twenty-first-century psychonauts—literally "sailors of the psyche"—seeking the most profound journey of all: the journey into inner space in order to discover self-realization and mystical union.

John Cunningham Lilly was born into a wealthy Minnesotan banking family on January 6, 1915, and, from a young age, showed a precocious talent for science. His nickname at prep school was Einstein Jr., and, after reading Sir James Jeans's *The Mysterious Universe*, he obsessed over the nature of the universe and the role of the mind in perceiving reality. While his peers were stealing kisses from girls and planning weekend outings, he wracked his brain in pursuit of deeper answers.

This deep-thinking began to bear fruit when, at the ripe-old age of sixteen, he wrote an amazingly evolved essay entitled "Reality," which explored subjective versus objective aspects of reality and the interplay of the mind within both. It soon became quite clear to all of his teachers and fellow students that this was *not* your typical teenager.

Disappointing his banker father, who had encouraged him to go to Harvard and pursue a career in business, the young John C. Lilly chose instead to attend the California Institute of Technology, where he received a full scholarship and hoped to study physics. However, after reading Aldous Huxley's *Brave New World* in 1934, he shifted his academic interests at Caltech from physics to biology as he became interested in the role that technology might play in furthering human potential. Eventually, this interest would lead him to study medicine at Dartmouth College and to eventually

continued

receive his medical degree from the University of Pennsylvania in 1942. Although he initially did research on human physiology (specifically, research related to the effects of high-altitude flying on the human body), he became more interested in consciousness research after World War II, when he trained in psychoanalysis at the University of Pennsylvania.

Intrigued by notions of the psyche and the role of the physical structures of the brain on human consciousness, he began doing research for the National Institute of Mental Health (NIMH) during the early 1950s; it was during this period that he first developed what came to be known as a sensory-deprivation or flotation tank.

Lilly had discovered that the bulk of the human brain was devoted to processing the vast amounts of sensory data that our five senses were constantly inputting. He felt that by stripping away all of this outside stimuli, the brain's capacity could be freed up, like hard-drive space on a computer, in order to apprehend deeper levels of consciousness and reality. Using himself as the test subject, Lilly became a pioneering psychonaut, experientially exploring previously uncharted waters of the human psyche.

He developed an understanding of the brain-mind-body relationship that can be a very useful model as we explore Greek metaphysical enlightenment. In his 1972 book *Programming the Human BioComputer*, he describes the human body as a "biochemical robot—a computer" that is, like any computer, programmed; in his conception, some of these programs are hardwired at birth, while others are "metaprograms" that are learned. He felt that what limits our

continued

How Plato and Pythagoras Can Save Your Life

capacities as human beings are our beliefs and "meta-beliefs" regarding what we're capable of and, indeed, what the very nature of reality is. His key insight is that we can self-program ourselves if we understand this dynamic; in his later book *The Steersman*, he describes how we can effectively take the helm of our biocomputer to override the "what we can't do" limitations that we've all been taught and allow our consciousness to break free and discover other as-yet-unexplored layers of reality that are embedded within the human psyche.

Lilly's books are some of the most interesting and insightful works ever written about the inner space of human consciousness. This is how *Psychology Today* describes his research and insights: "If there is a cartographer of altered states of consciousness—of the highways and byways of the inner trip—it is John Lilly, a rare combination of scientist and mystic."

As someone who has tried the flotation tanks that Lilly so passionately felt could kick open Huxley's "doors of perception," I can say that they are indeed the Royal Road towards greater awareness. For that reason, they are my very highly recommended gold standard for a modern-day version of the ancient Greek incubation.

The caveat? Well, as a person who knows a bit about addiction, I'm very cognizant of exploring non-pharmaceutically aided altered states of consciousness. Lilly? Not so much. As I mentioned, he aided his metaphysical quest with heavy doses of LSD and ketamine. I personally don't recommend either of those additions. While in transpersonal psychology there is a rich history of what's called entheogenic research (*entheogenic* literally means "into God" and is the field of study

continued

that explores psychedelic research), it is fraught with dangerous outcomes. In my opinion, natural or pharmaceutical substances are, quite simply, entirely unnecessary for the ultimate mind trip. You can trip the light fantastic drug free!

Lilly's personal story itself is a powerful testament of those dangers; his is the story of a man who played with fire and got burned. His ketamine use became so frequent that he would spend hour after hour injecting himself with ketamine and floating in his tank; in one almost-catastrophic incident, he was saved from drowning in his own tank by the fervent CPR efforts of his wife after he had lost consciousness and turned blue. Lilly's addiction to this mind-altered state can serve as warning that all pleasant—even ecstatic—states have addictive potential.

Indeed, during the thirteenth century, followers of the mystic Sufi poet Rumi would dance and spin around a pole in order to achieve an ecstatic state; these spinning mystics were known as whirling dervishes (a great fun fact for *Trivial Pursuit*). But inevitably there were those whirling dervishes that couldn't stop spinning; the state they had achieved simply felt so good that they would spin without eating or resting until they eventually collapsed from exhaustion. Interestingly, the Sufis had a name for these spinning-addicted dervishes: spiritual drunkards. Perhaps it is fair to say that Lilly became a ketamine-injecting and floating spiritual drunkard.

What can we learn from this? Metaphysical seeker beware: seek, explore, transcend, but remain tethered to this plane of reality and know when too much of a good thing may become a bad thing.

Exercise 12

Incubation
(or How Death Can Transform Your Life)

This contemplative exercise is **a reenactment of an ancient *incubation* (a.k.a., death) ritual.** This meditation **can take anywhere from ninety minutes to several hours**; it is up to you to determine what length of time you feel comfortable with.

It is suggested that you use for this meditation a dark, quiet room where there is a sofa or bed that you can lie down in and where you know that you won't be disturbed. It is also suggested that you arrange to have a friend or aide to check in with you as the mediation progresses.

Some might prefer a more authentic incubation setting and opt for an actual cave; for others who may have the resources, a sensory-deprivation tank is probably the gold standard in incubation vehicles (see "Breaking Free From the Cage via Altered States: Flotation Tanks and Dr. John C. Lilly").

Before beginning the incubation, read this preceding chapter in its entirety. Then read the following passage:

> The source of light is at home in the darkness . . . the point where day and night both come out from the mythical place where earth and heaven have their source . . . . Death for us seems just nothingness, where we have to leave everything behind. But it's also a fullness that can hardly be conceived of, where everything is in contact with everything and nothing is ever lost. And yet to know that, you have to be able to become conscious in the world of the dead.

During the incubation, contemplate these questions: What is being? What is nonbeing?

When you're done with your incubation, immediately write down what emerged for you during this process. Please write everything that arises within your conscious awareness. Then sit for several more moments and become aware of how you feel. Finally, look around the room; do you experience it any differently than you did before you began?

PART SIX

Yes, But . . . What Does It All Mean?

ᕦᕦᕦᕦᕦᕦᕦᕦᕦᕦ

The most beautiful thing we can experience is the mysterious. It is the source of all true art and all science. He to whom this emotion is a stranger, who can no longer pause to wonder and stand rapt in awe, is as good as dead: his eyes are closed.

—Albert Einstein

Your vision will become clear only when you look into your heart. Who looks outside, dreams. Who looks inside, awakens.

—Carl Jung

Don't go back to sleep.

—Rumi

A ship is safe in harbor, but that's not what ships are for.

—William Shedd

16

New Science and Old Wisdom

Science is a funny thing. We think that we know something until we realize that, well, maybe, we don't really know that something, or at least maybe we don't fully understand that something as much as we thought we did.

It's just the nature of the beast; scientists develop a theory that they think explains something, and it may very well explain everything that's known up until that point. But then an unusual blip occurs—an outlier—that can't be explained by the existing theory. So then what do you have? Answer: a worthless theory. Because if a theory or a "law" of science can't explain every instance of a phenomenon that it attempts to explain, then it's not really worth the paper that it's written on.

Take the law of gravity. We are told that objects with a large mass generate a gravitational field that pulls objects downwards. If, however, we were to encounter a gravitational anomaly—say, for example, we were to discover an apple that "fell" upwards out of a tree rather than downwards—what then? We might be forced to conclude that perhaps we don't understand this thing we call gravity as well as we think we do because the law of gravity doesn't explain *all* of the available data. In other words, we would be forced to reevaluate the worldview that embraces gravity as a law, and be forced to seek an alternate, more comprehensive explanation for why that one apple falls upwards.

Make no mistake, science is full of examples of apples falling upwards. New theories are constantly replacing older, more obsolete theories as blips and outliers shatter old paradigms and necessitate new perspectives. For example, in physics, classical mechanics (such as Newton's ideas about gravity) were replaced (or supplemented) by theories of relativity (Einstein's little $E=MC^2$ formula), which then were made somewhat obsolete by quantum mechanics. This evolution of theories has not only been true in physics, but also in other fields, such as astronomy, the biological sciences, and mathematics.

And what about our ideas about what it means to be human? How have they evolved? Well, from a Western perspective, we've gone from Adam and Eve creationism to enlightenment-period notions of a "ghost in the machine" (Descartes' view of a physical body with an animating life force) to present-day materialist ideas of biological reductionism (chemicals wrapped in skin). But are there any outliers—are there any apples falling upwards—to refute biological reductionism?

Luckily, yes. Earlier in this book, I had discussed the William James notion of white crows and the truly exceptional abilities of a handful of very gifted people that seem to push the boundary of human potential. There are other anomalies that are difficult, if not impossible, to explain via the mainstream scientific theories and paradigms. What are some of these head scratchers?

- William Tiller and his team at Stanford have conducted repeatable experiments wherein properties of a material object (in this case, the pH level of a sample of water) were impacted (the pH level was either raised or lowered) by focused meditative thought.

- Charles Tart, a research psychologist at the University of California, Davis, constructed an experiment wherein a woman who had claimed to have out-of-body experiences (OBEs) was monitored in a controlled sleep laboratory and connected to an electroencephalogram (EEG). During rapid-eye-movement (REM) sleep, she was able to "see" a randomly selected five-digit number that had been placed on a high shelf near the ceiling, accurately reciting the number upon awakening. The probability of her guessing the correct number was approximately 1 in 100,000.

- Indiana University biologist Paul Pietsch taught salamanders new ways to feed and then experimented with removing their brains. (Salamanders can briefly survive in a stupor state without a brain.) He then replaced their brains after he had performed over 700 different variations of flip-flopping, slicing, shuffling, and even mincing the little brains. In each case, the salamander would return to normal and resume its learned feeding behavior. Pietsch concluded that his experiments seemed to contradict mainstream neuroscience's pervading assumption that memories and/or learning were localized in any one particular part of the brain.

- Computer scientist Simon Berkovitch calculated that in order to produce and store a lifetime's worth of experiences, the brain would have to carry out 10 to the 24th order of operations per second. But Dutch neurobiologist Herms Romijn has shown that this would be impossible even if *all* 100 billion neurons in the brain were involved (which they are not, since there are only 20 billion neurons in the cerebral cortex). So where—and how—do we produce and store our lifetime of experiences?

• Neuropsychologist Paul Pearsall chronicles the case of an eight-year old girl who had received the transplanted heart of a murdered ten-year-old girl and then began having vivid nightmares of her donor's murder. The nightmares were so clear that the young girl was able to describe not only the murderer, but also the clothes that he was wearing on the night of the murder, the weapon that he used, the place that the horrific attack had occurred, and even what the murderer told the little girl before she died. All these details were confirmed by police, and the murderer was arrested and eventually convicted. It seemed that the organ recipient had somehow absorbed some "organ memory" from her donor, yet this is not considered possible by mainstream science.

And there are many more examples of apples falling upwards—in physics and in consciousness research (as we'll further discuss)—but why are they important? In our earlier discussion of white crows, I mentioned that the notion of white crows requires us to reconceptualize how we view our human capacities. These paradigm-busters open up the door to the *possibility* of our *possibilities*. I made the point that to reflexively slam shut the door on even allowing that such unusual abilities might be possible precludes us from being able to push the boundary of our own potential. Similarly, these apples falling upwards, these outliers and anomalies from the natural world and the physical sciences, also force us to reevaluate our existing paradigms.

Any book that attempts to honor Pythagoras and other Greek mystics by helping people to experience deeper levels of reality—and thus pulling the existential rug out from under people—has to provide alternative paradigms to replace the old, shattered ones. It is thus essential to provide the theoretical framework that can allow for the possibility of such mind-expanding capabilities. In order to help engender an open mind-set towards such paradigm-busting possibilities, I'd like to briefly describe some more of the discoveries of the new science, as well as some of the various "new-paradigm" theories that might be able to theoretically explain how some of these anomalies might be possible.

What are some of the scientific developments of the new science of the last century that may have relevance in a discussion about the metaphysical, unseen reality that Pythagoras and Plato believed existed in a causal informational realm (what Plato called the Ideal Realm)? Interestingly, yet on somewhat of a sidenote, even main-stream physicists now commonly refer to matter as "information," since they believe that "information is more fundamental than matter" (Radin 2006). And where does this new science begin?

Most of the advances I am referring to first began developing during the dawn of the last century, when advancements in the realm of the subatomic rocked the very foundation of what has been called classical mechanics or Newtonian physics. These experiments undermined the notion that all of reality is built of blocks that are themselves indivisible. What scientists discovered was that the subatomic particles that emerged when atoms and atomic nuclei were fissioned did not behave like conventional solids. Instead, they displayed an odd, paradoxically dual nature, alternately exhibiting wavelike or particlelike properties that were inexplicably determined by the mode of observation.

Danish physicist Niels Bohr, acknowledged as one of the founding fathers of quantum physics, pointed out that if subatomic particles only come into existence in the presence of an observer, then it would be meaningless to speak of particles' properties as existing before they are observed. This conclusion troubled one of the other founders of quantum theory, Albert Einstein. As troubling as these implications were on a subatomic level, Einstein refused to believe that they could have any implication on a larger, macro level; for example, he just thought it ludicrous to imply that, say, a cat did not exist until someone actually looked at it.

In 1935, Einstein and two associates, Boris Podolsky and Nathan Rosen, published a now-famous paper that discussed what has come to be known as the Einstein-Podolsky-Rosen Paradox. Their paper was entitled "Can Quantum-Mechanical Description of Physical Reality Be Considered Complete?" and was written as a refutation of what Einstein described as "spooky action at a distance."

Yet later, precise research would indeed validate Bohr's original insights. The cat didn't disappear if it wasn't observed, but Bohr's ideas did seem to very accurately predict and describe phenomena in the infinitesimal and unseen-to-the-naked-eye subatomic realm.

Further phenomena, dubbed by physicist Erwin Schrodinger as *entanglement*, were also discovered. Entanglement was the ability of certain separated particles to instantaneously influence one another in what has been called a *nonlocal* effect. This influence indicates a seeming state of connectedness between particles, even when those particles have been separated across space and time.

In the 1960s, Irish physicist John Bell became the first researcher to construct a theoretical laboratory experiment to confirm the entanglement phenomenon. When, in the 1980s, Bell's theory was experimentally confirmed, the phenomenon became known as Bell's Theorem of Nonlocality. In these later and very precise experiments, two "sister" electrons were separated across a certain distance and were no longer in physical contact with one another. When the rotational spin of one electron was artificially manipulated to change direction (for example, from clockwise to counterclockwise), the rotational spin of the sister electron across the room would also *instantaneously* change rotation. This result was not only remarkable but, according to Newtonian physics, should have been impossible. There was no physical or observable means by which the one electron was communicating or sending information to the other electron indicating a shift in rotation.

Yet shift they did.

These nonlocality results have since been repeated hundreds of times in very precise experiments that have only further affirmed Bell's original theory. These results are so indisputable in the scientific community, that quantum nonlocality and entanglement are today accepted doctrines of mainstream science.

While these phenomena may be undisputed in the micro subatomic realm, many physicists have continued to debate whether or not entanglement and nonlocality effects exist at the macro level. But recent research findings may be forcing scientists to reconsider their stance on this. In a review of developments on entanglement research, as quoted by science writer Michael Brooks in Dean Radin's *Entangled Minds* (2006), "Physicists now believe that entanglement between particles exists everywhere, all the time, and have recently found shocking evidence that it affects the wider, 'macroscopic' world that we inhabit." Many paranormal researchers point towards quantum discoveries as possible explanatory frameworks for anomalous experiences, such as various psychic phenomena, also known as *psi phenomena*.

Then there are the holographic theories. Physicist David Bohm, based on his earlier observation and research at the

Lawrence Berkeley National Laboratory (a.k.a., Berkeley Lab), noticed certain collective and seemingly interconnected properties of plasma gas that led him to seek a more satisfying explanation than Bohr's interpretation. He believed that there was a deeper reality beyond the absence of observers. He proposed a new field theory called the *quantum potential* and theorized that it pervaded all space. Years later, after observing the properties of ink in glycerin, Bohm hypothesized a radical new theory to explain what he felt was a better model for reality's implicate (unseen) and explicate (seen) order: the universe as a hologram.

In a hologram, what is visually seen is a sort of three-dimensional interference-pattern projection that has a causal higher light or laser source. Thus, a laser creates a three-dimensional hologram from the information contained on a two-dimensional surface. In addition, all the information for the hologram is contained in that other implicate causal plane, which then informs and becomes explicate in the form of the three-dimensional hologram (Talbot 1991).

One of the most interesting properties of a hologram that can lend a theoretical framework for certain phenomena such as archetypal experiences, encounters with the collective unconscious, and other unusual phenomena that have emerged from consciousness studies is the "whole in every part" aspect of a hologram. What this aspect means is that within every subset of the explicate, or seen, part of the hologram, lays the implicate, or unseen, information—the DNA, if you will—of the entire hologram. This model gives new meaning to the old line from the William Blake poem "to see a world in a grain of sand."

Separately and independently from Bohm, neurophysiologist Karl Pribram also developed a holographic model to explain certain properties of memories. Pribram's model indicates that perhaps memories were not localized within any particular specific brain site, but seemingly distributed throughout the brain as a whole. Pribram concluded that aspects of "mind" lent themselves to explanation via a holographic brain model, which he went on to propose in the 1970s after various experiments (such as Pietsch's salamander experiment) seemed to support his theory.

Pribram wondered if, in fact, what the mystics had been saying for centuries might be true—that reality might indeed be an illusion, and that what was really out there was just a vast, "resonating symphony of wave forms." Otherwise known as a *frequency domain*, that waveform symphony was transformed into the material world as we know it only after it entered our senses.

As one can readily see, there are obvious parallels between a holographic model of the universe and Plato's notions of causal Ideal Realms or Pythagoras's informational realm. And there was yet more evidence from the world of theoretical astrophysics suggesting that the universe might indeed be a hologram; it came from the "information paradox" of black holes that Stephen Hawking pointed to over three decades ago.

This paradox begins with two facts: (1) the immense gravity of black holes sucks in all surrounding information (in the forms of matter and energy) and (2) black holes have been mathematically shown to eventually collapse in on themselves and disappear. The question is, what happens to all that sucked-in information when the black holes collapse? If it too were to disappear, that disappearance would contradict some of the most fundamental laws of physics.

For over thirty years, Hawking stuck to his belief that black holes did indeed destroy information. This was in spite of the fact that something that has been dubbed "Hawking radiation" emanates out of the black hole. Hawking argued that this radiation was random and could not contain the information that had originally fallen into the hole.

But in 1997, Juan Maldacena of the Institute for Advanced Study in Princeton, New Jersey, developed a type of string theory in a universe with five large dimensions of space and a contorted space-time geometry. In his theory, which also included gravity, everything happening on the boundary (the event horizon) of the black hole is equivalent to everything happening inside the black hole; that is, ordinary particles interacting on the surface of the black hole correspond exactly to strings interacting on the interior of the black hole—sort of like a hologram. According to his theory, a black hole, like everything else in the universe, has an alter ego living on the boundary of the universe. Shockingly (at least for Hawking) Maldacena's theory suggested that "our universe might be something of a grand illusion—an enormous cosmic hologram" (Minkel, "The Hollow Universe," *New Scientist* 2002, 22). This suggestion, again, corresponds to Plato's causal Ideal Realm or Pythagoras's informational realm.

Maldacena's calculations were so impeccable, his theory so elegant, that in 2004, at a conference in Dublin, Hawking conceded he had been wrong about information loss in a black hole.

According to Stanford physicist Leonard Susskind, credited as one of the inventors of string theory, Maldacena's theory was "so mathematically precise that for most practical purposes all theoretical physicists came to the conclusion that the holographic principle and the conservation of information would have to be true" (Gefter, "The Elephant and the Event Horizon," *New Scientist* 2006).

In addition to physics research, consciousness research has also yielded discoveries that have defied explanation by the standard scientific models. Thought and consciousness (and not just atomic particles) have demonstrated nonlocal properties of entanglement.

Further, rigorous and repeatable experiments have explored a phenomenon known as direct mental interactions with living systems (DMILS). These experiments have yielded statistically significant data regarding people's abilities to influence the following systems via their thoughts and/or intentions (Braud 2003):

- the rate of hemolysis in human red-blood cells (hemolysis is death by osmotic stress);

- other people's sympathetic, autonomic nervous systems, as indicated by changes in electrical activity in the others' skin (measured by galvanic skin responses, or what is called allobiofeedback);

- the odd- or even-number output of computers, called random-number generators (a.k.a., Eggs), that were used in Princeton-based experiments (Radin 2006).

In addition, a controlled double-blind experiment has shown that intercessory prayer (healing prayer at a distance) yields positive recovery outcomes for coronary patients (Byrd 1998). There is also mounting evidence for other types of nonlocal human entanglement in the form of remote viewing (as was discussed in chapter 3), as well as less exotic forms of telepathy (Radin 2006; Targ 2004).

Besides holographic theories, another conceptualization that borrows from ancient wisdom is also gaining much traction within the scientific community. Systems theorist and visionary author Ervin Laszlo has proposed an Akashic Field theory that borrows from the Hindu concept of the Akashic Record. *Akashic* is a Sanskrit word that literally means "sky" or "aether," but is used to describe the belief in a cosmic record of all that has ever occurred; this concept has also variously been called the collective consciousness or cosmic mind. In Laszlo's version, the Akashic is a subquantum field containing the holographic record of everything that happens—or has happened—in the universe. Laszlo illustrates his theory with a sea analogy. Anything that moves through the sea leaves a vibration in the water in the form of a wake. The Akashic Field is like the sea, and any object or happening leaves a similar vibration in it; that vibration is the record of that particular object or event.

Taken in its totality, Laszlo's A-Field (as it is also known) represents the embodiment of the philosophy known as Monistic Idealism, which is the school of philosophy that believes that everything is consciousness and that what we perceive as matter is, instead, just various ripples in the A-field vibrating in such a way that they take on the *appearance* of shape and form.

According to MIT physicist Milo Wolf, Laszlo's A-field is the cosmic vacuum or the "wave medium" in which all the material universe—particles, stars, people, planets—are not material. Instead, as Laszlo says, "[A]ll of these *matter-like* things are complex waves in the quantum vacuum."

It should then be theoretically possible to entrain one's frequency to resonate with the larger A-Field. Or, as Apollo 14 Captain Edgar Mitchell describes it, "[I]n higher states of awareness, every cell of the body coherently resonates with the holographically embedded information in the quantum zero-point energy field." (Mitchell had a mystical experience on the moon and went on to found the Institute of Noetic Sciences, or IONS.)

Recall our earlier discussion from chapter 2 regarding water meditation and entrainment; it would seem that if a person can reach a higher level of awareness through a variety of different practices (including Greek contemplative meditation), access to these higher informational realms becomes possible. And when these higher realms are accessed, the white-crow abilities demonstrated by people such as the calendrical savants or Pat Price (the remote viewer) become less unexplainable and paranormal and, instead, become both comprehensible and quite *possible*.

But Laszlo makes an important observation about accessing such "quantum-brain" abilities. In analyzing savants, he explains that they—due to their autism—preferentially use the right hemisphere of the brain; in other words, they experience things in visual terms. Laszlo suggests that perhaps the brain has two modes: One is the classic slow and linear problem-solving mode (the left-hemisphere-based thinking brain). The other is what he calls the *quantum-processing* mode; this mode is extremely rapid, capable of handling exponentially more information than the classical mode. It is the right-hemisphered brain that Laszlo suggests is in contact with the holographic informational field and is thus able to receive those lightning bolts of transcendent inspiration.

What's the catch? It seems that the quantum-processing mode only kicks in when the classical-processing mode is deactivated. That would explain why the altered states produced by various types of meditation are so effective; in the altered states, the left-hemisphere, classical-processing brain is turned off. The same thing happens with my exercise-before-contemplation technique; the physical exhaustion shuts down the thinking brain.

It also explains the mechanism by which people in sensory-deprivation tanks often have mystical experiences. In this modern form of Greek incubation, once the sensory input data ceases to stimulate the classical-processing mode of the brain, that mode is deactivated, and the quantum-processing mode is activated—and thus able to tap into the holographic archetypal realm.

In his groundbreaking book *The Biology of Transcendence* (2002), Joseph Chilton Pearce discusses a concept known as "unconflicted behavior" (a concept we had briefly discussed earlier). Unconflicted behavior is a mental state of *being* that is unburdened by doubt or overthinking. It is, in essence, a very unforced and uncomplicated way of thinking; in fact, this way of thinking is rather simple and childlike (and is symptomatic of most savants). Is this unconflicted behavior the same as the non-right hemisphere approach that Laszlo describes, or is it a different dynamic altogether?

Pearce describes how during such unconflicted states, one is able to think and do things on an almost superhuman level. The unconflicted person seems to be in direct contact with a transcendent source. The difficulty for most people, Pearce noted, was in *maintaining* that pure, unconflicted state. Yet savants, by virtue of cognitive limitation coupled with an enhanced ability to focus, can blissfully maintain this seemingly effortless and unconflicted mental state; thus, they seem almost uniquely able to maintain an "open channel."

Pearce goes on to cite the legendary 1962 book by Marghanita Laski, *Ecstasy: A Study of Some Secular and Religious Experiences*, published by Indiana University Press. In it, she describes her research of "Eureka!" breakthrough types of experiences in the fields of science, philosophy, art, and religion. She was able to identify six common themes that were uniformly present for such seemingly transcendent phenomena to occur. Briefly stated, all of those who experienced such moments had:

1. Asked a question; something was passionately sought.

2. Searched for the answer; this entailed rigorous exploration.

How Plato and Pythagoras Can Save Your Life

3. Hit a plateau; total stagnation was reached with no progress, despite total dedication.

4. Given up all hope; the person quit the quest entirely.

5. Eventually experienced a breakthrough (but *only* after giving up).

6. Translated the answer into the common domain. Usually the answer arrived fully formed, and time and effort was required to make sense of it.

Again, a similar precondition in Laski's study seemed to be the unconflicted mental state that seekers had assumed out of sheer mental exhaustion and frustration after quitting their trek—a level of fatigue and exhaustion that, interestingly, is similar to the *physical* exhaustion induced by my exercise-then-contemplate method. According to Laski's research, only when the seekers were exhausted and had quit searching for an answer did the seemingly transcendent information appear, as Pearce describes it, like a fully formed lightning bolt in the seekers' conscious awareness.

And it seems that, as with lightning, the necessary ground charge needs to be created in the recipient. In Laski's subjects, this ground charge would seem to be the fervent effort put forth by the seekers, even though the solution eluded them in the actively thinking, left-hemisphere-dominant state. They seem to have effectively created the necessary receptive charge, but only *after* they had stopped seeking. It would seem that while they were still actively seeking, their "thinking," left-hemisphere brain was still activated and acting as a barrier to Laszlo's quantum-processing brain. Once that side of the brain was shut down out of frustration, the information-accessing, quantum-processing right hemisphere could turn on. That *quitting* seemed to be the final piece necessary to create the unconflicted, right-hemisphere mental state that would allow the lightning to strike. We might speculate that by attaining an unconflicted mind-set, by meditative practice or contemplation (and/or physical exhaustion!), one can create the ground charge needed for transcendent lightning to strike from that beyond realm we've been calling Pythagoras's Informational Realm or Plato's Ideal Realm.

Perhaps that's how Pythagoras was able to hear the universe vibrating or was able to remember his past lives. Perhaps that's how mystics can intuit cosmological insights and how psychics and clairvoyants can see things. Perhaps they're all able to achieve a form of unconflicted transcendence, or a right-hemisphere, quantum-processing mode.

And if the white crows can do it, then so can you!

How Plato and Pythagoras Can Save Your Life

17

Musings From My Dissertation

As it was designed for my study, my Greek-inspired contemplative method was a three-pronged technique. It involved (1) weekly philosophical readings, (2) guided, weekly transrational contemplative meditations based on that week's readings, and (3) forty-minute dialectical discussion groups led by me as facilitator.

This book's chapters on Pythagoras, Plato, and Parmenides are distilled from the weekly philosophical readings my participants had to do for my study, so those chapters can serve as the readings for anyone pursuing my method on their own. The twelve guided mediations (the exercises) throughout the book closely mirror the contemplative meditations that were done in the study. These meditations could be done over several days or weeks, or they can be done periodically as the reader feels necessary.

As the contemplations on the nature of reality progress, the movement of the meditations continues to expand outward from the rational (meditations on mathematics and the cosmos) to the transrational (logic paradoxes and quantum effects). This progression starts with Pythagoras and Plato and concludes with the most mystical session, a recreation of the incubation—"death before dying."

This final incubation session can last anywhere from ninety minutes to several hours. For it, you can use a dark and quiet room or, if you want to go old school, an actual, honest-to-goodness cave. For those who have the means and the access, a sensory-deprivation tank is highly suggested. But again, if you can't find a cave or get your hands on a sense-dep tank, then a dark and quiet room will do the trick.

As part of the incubation, you are asked to first read a certain passage from the ancients regarding the nature of being. (That passage is included in the instructions for exercise 12.) During the incubation, you are to contemplate the very nature of existence and "beingness," as well as being the nature of non-being, or what some might call death.

When my study participants and I performed the incubation sessions, we experienced an almost surreal sense of consciousness expansion. Powerful imagery, unusual insights, a sense of equanimity—all of these things were reported during these sessions. It was pretty heavy-duty stuff.

I also strongly encourage readers who undergo the incubation process to write down their thoughts and experiences immediately afterward. These records are extremely helpful to further the process and integrate this profound experience.

Overall, my research subjects indicated that they experienced a real benefit in immersing themselves in the Greek miracle. They indicated that they had more of a sense of purpose in their lives, felt more connected, experienced an increased sense of concern for others, and felt an increased sense of spirituality, as well as a greater concern with social or planetary values. These effects were measured both qualitatively and quantitatively via standardized assessment tools.

I have included here the abstract from my study; it describes the methods I used, the participants, and the quite successful results that we were able to achieve. In fact, because of those results, I was asked to present my research findings at the 2007 American Psychological Association (APA) annual conference in San Francisco.

My Dissertation Abstract

Beyond Reason: Transrational Contemplation and Greek Mystical Philosophy

By Nicholas Kardaras

The researcher hypothesized that participants engaged in a method informed by Greek mystical philosophy could experience measurable increases in their levels of personal or transpersonal awareness. Thematic Content Analysis, Narrative Analysis, and statistically significant *t*-tests all confirmed the hypothesis that the *Methodos Philosophia* could increase levels of awareness.

Participants described meaningfully increased levels of personal as well as transpersonal levels of awareness, and the Greyson/Ring Life Changes Inventory-Revised (LCI-R) yielded statistically significant increases in values associated with an appreciation for life as well as death, a quest for meaning or a sense of purpose, concern for others, spirituality, self-acceptance, and a concern with social or planetary values.

Metaphysical ancient Greek philosophers had emphasized an almost-forgotten integral practice of deep transrational contemplation by which they used the rational,

continued

---

reasoning mind as a key to unlock the noetic awareness of the higher Mind. These mystical philosophers ranged their contemplations along a broad spectrum of subjects such as cosmology, mathematics, philosophy, and music.

Ancient Greek philosophers such as Pythagoras, Plato, and Plotinus believed that such contemplative meditations could have profound consciousness-expanding effects wherein the individual could have a deeper, more direct awareness of personal and cosmological reality.

For this study, the researcher developed a modern contemplative method, the *Methodos Philosophia*, which was an interpretive revisioning of Greek philosophical mystical contemplation. This 3-step method involved participants doing weekly readings, engaging in weekly dialectically active group discussions wherein the assigned readings were discussed, and then sitting for a guided contemplative meditation.

Twelve persons (six males and six females), ranging in age from twenty-three to sixty-seven and of varying spiritual and transpersonal temperaments, participated over an eight-week period in a mixed-methods study that examined the experience as well as the accompaniments and outcomes of the practice of this contemplative method.

The researcher collected four types of data: weekly qualitative questionnaires, post study semi-structured interviews, phenomenologically informed weekly interviews, and a post only standardized assessment of life changes (LCI-R).

18

Some Final Thoughts

And so here it is. We're close to the end of the book—a book that some of you may have found interesting or exciting, or perhaps others may have found rather odd. You may have thought, quite justifiably, what kind of strange book is this? We have a book primarily about Greek mystical philosophy with an autobiographical intro that includes nightclub stories, recollections of all sorts of nocturnal candy along with a story about death and transformation and some explorations into new science. What gives?

Well, in many ways, writing this book was the culmination of my very own twenty-year odyssey; the synchronicity of seeing that old boat named *The Odyssey* when I was at a crossroads was quite powerful for me. The universe kept calling me back to my ancestral roots; I just felt compelled to turn people on to some of the ideas of the world's great thinkers, which had helped me to experience the world and the universe in such a fuller and more satisfying way than I had before. My rather *extreme* personal story was the honey to lure people into the book, so I could then expose them to the wondrous, consciousness-expanding ideas of people like Pythagoras, Plato, and William James.

And why do I think that's important? While the old axiom "you are what you eat" may be true, the ancient Greeks and I believe that you are also what you think. Contemplations on things such as math, music, philosophy, and cosmology have a way of elevating one's level of consciousness in ways more permanent than any mind-altering substance could ever achieve. It's my contention that the contents of our mind, as well as the subject of our thoughts, inform who we are, so that we indeed become what we think.

Think about this: if you immerse yourself in playing a violent video game like *Grand Theft Auto* for four hours a day instead of listening to classical music while engaging in informed discussions on the evolution of the universe for those same four hours, what might the impact be?

I suggest that the content and focus of our thoughts and intentions does more than impact us; they actually inform us and, thus, actually shape who we are. We are either elevated or debased by our thoughts and endeavors.

And what I'm talking about here is more than just molding our behaviors. We all know that kids who are desensitized to violence are more apt to engage in violence. What I'm talking about is actually affecting us on a cellular, spiritual-DNA level. To use Pythagoras's Music of the Spheres vibrational language, our thinking tunes our frequencies and causes us to resonate in an entirely different way. We, thus, actually vibrate differently. So we really do become what we think. In fact, Pythagoras believed that if you contemplated something like infinity, you would actually *become* infinite. So what do we become when we contemplate something ugly or debasing?

Certainly in a culture where most people's thoughts are focused on the empty preoccupations of shopping, or video games, or *American Idol*, a society where most people tend to be anxious and angry, there may be a need for the voices of the long-dead ancient Greek philosophers to come alive again to help us understand that what we think matters—that ideas and beauty and ethics and philosophy both *form* and *shape* us.

Let's nurture our thinking so that it elevates not only us as individuals, but also the larger collective soup that we're swimming in.

Can I prove that thoughts impact the world? Not exactly, but the evidence and data for those who choose to look at it seems to support that, in statistically significant ways, there does seem to be something interesting going on. And while some may question whether thoughts can impact the external world, I think there's little doubt that one's thinking can certainly affect one's own life.

As for me, I'll choose to hitch my beliefs to the wagon of some of humanity's greatest thinkers: Pythagoras, Plato, Parmenides, Plotinus, William James, Carl Jung, Albert Einstein, Neils Bohr, David Bohm, Huston Smith, Ervin Laszlo, and Joseph Chilton Pearce, amongst others. What else can I say other than I'm very grateful these days that I can look in the mirror and not have to avoid eye contact. Today, I can look into my twin sons' eyes and know that I'm living the kind of life that they can be proud of. I know that my journey has been pretty extreme. In fact, I think that I might be the only person that's ever gone from being a Manhattan nightclub owner to becoming a Ph.D. and college professor. It's strange; in writing *How Plato and Pythagoras Can Save Your Life*, I kept having this odd feeling that the only reason I survived all my close encounters with death was so that I could complete this book. I really hope that it can provide some tangible, practical ways that people can use if they genuinely want a more engaged and meaningful life. I know that I try to the best of my ability to embrace the *Bios Pythagorikos* that I've described in the book: I don't drink or smoke. I eat well. I exercise regularly. I try and live as ethically and honestly as I can. I do contemplative meditations and am constantly looking up at the night sky in wonder. And, in the process, my life is amazingly full, and I'm a truly happy camper.

So if you're not happy with certain things in your life, why not change them? If you're not happy with *yourself*, then change that too! Apply the alchemy of Pythagoras and Plato as I did to transform yourself and to elevate your game. As I mentioned, the Greeks may have had a bit of a preoccupation with death and death rituals, but that was so that they could transform themselves into their fullest, most actualized self.

So may the universe be with you, as I hope that you join me in the Alchemy Survivors' Club!

References

Works Cited

Byrd, Randolph. "Positive Therapeutic Effects of Intercessory Prayer in a Coronary Care Unit Population." *Southern Medical Journal* 81, no. 7 (July 1988): 826–829.

Braud, William. *Distant Mental Influence: Its Contributions to Science, Healing and Human Interactions.* Charlottesville, VA: Hampton Roads, 2003.

Gefter, Amanda. "The Elephant and the Event Horizon." *New Scientist* no. 2575 (Oct. 26, 2006): 36-39.

Hoffman, David, and Sharon Hoffman. "Enigma, Paradox, Parable." *Parabola: Myth, Tradition, and the Search for Meaning* 25, no. 2 (2000):14–17.

Kingsley, Peter. *In the Dark Places of Wisdom.* Inverness, CA: The Golden Sufi Center, 1999.

———. *Reality.* Inverness, CA: The Golden Sufi Center, 2004.

Magee, Bryan. *The Story of Thought: The Essential Guide to the History of Western Philosophy.* London: DK, 1998.

Markides, Kyriacos. *Fire in the Heart: Healers, Sages and Mystics.* New York: Penguin, 1992.

———. *The Magus of Stravolos: The Extraordinary World of a Spiritual Healer.* New York: Penguin, 1989.

————. *The Mountain of Silence: A Search for Orthodox Spiritual-ity.* New York: Doubleday, 2002.

Minkel, J. R. "The Hollow Universe." *New Scientist* 174, no. 2340 (April 27, 2002): 22.

Miranda, S. M. "St. Thomas Aquinas Forum." www.saintaquinas. com.

Radin, Dean. *Entangled Minds: Extrasensory Experiences in a Quantum Reality.* New York: Simon and Schuster, 2006.

Smith, Huston. *Why Religion Matters: The Fate of the Human Spirit in an Age of Disbelief.* New York: Harper Collins, 2001.

Talbot, Michael. *The Holographic Universe.* New York: Harper Collins, 1991.

Targ, Russell. *Limitless Mind: A Guide to Remote Viewing and Transformation of Consciousness.* Novato, CA: New World Library, 2004.

Additional References

Becker, Ernest. *The Denial of Death.* New York: Free Press, 1973.

Boulter, Carmen. *The Pyramid Code.* Five-part series. DVD. Kultur Video, 2009.

Brooks, Michael. "Entanglement: The Weirdest Link." *New Scientist*, no. 2440 (March 27, 2004).

Bucke, R. M. *Cosmic Consciousness: A Study in the Evolution of the Human Mind.* New York: Penguin Books, 1902/1991.

Campbell, Joseph. *The Hero with a Thousand Faces.* Princeton, NJ: Princeton University Press, 1949/1972.

Pearce, J. C. *The Biology of Transcendence.* Rochester, VT: Park Street Press, 2002.

————. *The Crack in the Cosmic Egg.* Rochester, VT: Park Street Press, 1983/2002.

How Plato and Pythagoras Can Save Your Life

————. *Evolution's End*. San Francisco: HarperOne, 1993.

Dawkins, Richard. *The God Delusion*. New York: Houghton Mifflin, Harcourt, 2006.

Goswami, Amit. *The Self-Aware Universe*. New York: Tarcher, 1995.

Greene, Brian. *The Fabric of the Cosmos*. New York: Vintage Books, 2004.

Hamer, Dean. *The God Gene*. New York: Doubleday, 2004.

Hitchens, Christopher. *God Is Not Great: How Religion Poisons Everything*. New York: Twelve Books, 2007.

Huxley, Aldous. *Brave New World*. New York: Harper Perennial, 1932/1998.

Iamblichus. *On the Pythagorean Life*, trans. Gillian Clark. Liverpool, England: Liverpool University Press, 1989.

Jeans, Sir James. *The Mysterious Universe*. Whitefish, MT: Kessinger, 1930/2007.

Laski, Marghanita. *Ecstasy: A Study of Some Secular and Religious Experiences*. Santa Barbara, CA: The Greenwood Publishing Group, 1968.

Laszlo, Ervin. *Science and the Akashic Field: An Integral Theory of Everything*. Rochester, VT: Inner Traditions Press, 2004.

Lilly, John C. *Programming and Metaprogramming the Human Biocomputer*. Berkeley, CA: Ronin, 1968/2004.

————. *The Steersman: Metabeliefs and Self-Navigation*. Berkeley, CA: Ronin, 2007.

Murphy, Michael, and James Redfield. *God and the Evolving Universe*. London: Bantam, 2003.

Nietzsche, Friedrich. *The Gay Science*. New York: Cambridge University Press, 1882/2001.

Pietsch, Paul. *Shufflebrain*. New York: Houghton Mifflin, 1981.

Plato. *Phaedo: Plato in Twelve Volumes*, trans. H. N. Fowler. Boston: Harvard University Press, 1966.

———. *The Republic*, trans. R. E. Allen. New Haven: Yale University Press, 2006.

Ranke-Heinemann, Uta. *Putting Away Childish Things*. San Francisco: Harper, 1995.

Russell, Bertrand. *A History of Western Philosophy*. New York: Touchstone, 1945/1967.

Sinetar, Marsha. *Ordinary People as Monks and Mystics*. Mahwah, NJ: Paulist, 1986.

Uzdavinys, Algis. *The Golden Chain: An Anthology of Pythagorean and Platonic Philosophy*. Bloomington, IN: World Wisdom, 2004.

Wade, Nicholas. *The Faith Instinct*. New York: Penguin, 2009.

Suggested Reading

Cheney, Sheldon. *Men Who Have Walked with God*. New York: Knopf, 1945.

Collinson, Diane. *Fifty Major Philosophers: A Study Guide*. London: Croom Helm, 1987.

Cornford, Francis Macdonald. *From Religion to Philosophy: A Study in the Origins of Western Speculation*. New York: Dover, 2004.

Deck, John. *Nature, Contemplation, and the One: A Study in the Philosophy of Plotinus*. New York: Larson, 1991.

Dodds, E. R. *The Greeks and the Irrational*. Berkeley: University of California Press, 1951.

Frost, S. E. *The Basic Teachings of the Great Philosophers*. New York: Doubleday, 1962.

Gall, Edward. *Mysticism Throughout the Ages*. New York: Kessinger, 1967.

Gifford-May, D., and N. L. Thompson. "'Deep States of

How Plato and Pythagoras Can Save Your Life

Meditation: Phenomelogical Reports of Experience." *Journal of Transpersonal Psychology* 26 (1994):117–38.

Guthrie, Kenneth Sylvan. *The Pythagorean Sourcebook and Library.* Grand Rapids, MI: Phanes Press, 1987.

Hadot, Pierre. *What is Ancient Philosophy?* trans. M. Chase. Boston: Harvard University Press, 2002.

Hines, Brian. *Return to the One: Plotinus's Guide to God-Realization.* Bloomington, IN: Unlimited, 2004.

Howard, Alex. *Philosophy for Counseling and Psychotherapy: Pythagoras to Postmodernism.* New York: Palgrave, 2000.

James, Jamie. *The Music of the Spheres: Music, Science and the Natural Order of the Universe.* New York: Copernicus Press, 1993.

James, William. *The Varieties of Religious Experience.* New York: New American Library, 1902/1958.

Jung, Carl Gustav. *The Basic Writings of C. G. Jung,* ed. V. S. De Laszlo. New York: The Modern Library, 1959.

McDonald, Kathleen. *How to Meditate: A Practical Guide.* Boston, MA: Wisdom, 1984.

Merton, Thomas. *Mystics and Zen Masters.* New York: Noonday Press, 1961.

———. *New Seeds of Contemplation.* New York: New Directions Books, 1962.

Osborne, Catherine. *Presocratic Philosophy: A Very Short Introduction.* London: Oxford University Press, 2004.

Osborne, Richard. *Philosophy for Beginners.* New York: Writers and Readers, 1992.

Riedweg, Christoph. *Pythagoras: His life, Teaching, and Influence.* Ithaca, NY: Cornell University Press, 2002.

Robinson, Daniel. *An Intellectual History of Psychology.* New York: Macmillan, 1976.

Ross, Nancy Wilson. *Three Ways of Asian Wisdom: Hinduism, Buddhism, Zen*. New York: Simon and Schuster, 1966.

Seckel, Al. *The Great Book of Optical Illusions*. Toronto, Canada: Firefly Books, 2002.

Talbot, Michael. *Mysticism and the New Physics*. New York: Penguin Books, 1993.

Walsh, Roger, and Frances Vaughan. *Paths Beyond Ego*. New York: Tarcher/Putnam, 1993.

Wheelwright, Phillip. *The Presocratics*. New York: Macmillan, 1966.

Wilber, Ken. *The Marriage of Sense and Soul*. New York: Random House, 1998.

Wulff, David. "Mystical Experience." in *Varieties of Anomalous Experience: Examining the Scientific Evidence*, ed. E. Cardena, S. Krippner, and S. J. Lynn, 397–440 (Washington, DC: American Psychological Association, 2000).

To Our Readers

Conari Press, an imprint of Red Wheel/Weiser, publishes books on topics ranging from spirituality, personal growth, and relationships to women's issues, parenting, and social issues. Our mission is to publish quality books that will make a difference in people's lives—how we feel about ourselves and how we relate to one another. We value integrity, compassion, and receptivity, both in the books we publish and in the way we do business.

Our readers are our most important resource, and we appreciate your input, suggestions, and ideas about what you would like to see published.

Visit our website *www.redwheelweiser.com* where you can subscribe to our newsletters and learn about our upcoming books, special offers, and free downloads.

You can also contact us at *info@redwheelweiser.com*.

Conari Press

An imprint of Red Wheel/Weiser, LLC
665 Third Street, Suite 400
San Francisco, CA 94107

PYTHAGORAS, Pih THAG oh rus